MORE TRUE STORIES

A BEGINNING READER

D1500995

by Sandra Heyer

Longman

Introduction

MORE TRUE STORIES is a high-beginning reader for students of English as a Second Language. It consists of 22 units centered around human-interest stories adapted from newspapers and magazines. The vocabulary and structures used in the stories are carefully controlled to match those of a typical beginning ESL course. At the same time all attempts have been made to keep the language natural.

PRE-READING.

A photograph introduces each unit. Pre-reading questions based on these photographs are suggested to motivate the students to read, to encourage predictions about the content of the reading, and to aid in understanding difficult vocabulary.

READING THE STORY.

A three-step process is suggested for reading the story. After the pre-reading activities, the students read the story silently two times, once without stopping, then stopping to circle new vocabulary.

When all the students have finished reading, the teacher clarifies the meaning of new vocabulary, perhaps making reference to the vocabulary exercises to encourage guessing vocabulary from context clues.

Finally the teacher reads the story aloud while the students follow along in their texts. Teachers should, of course, adapt whatever reading strategies best suit their classes.

THE EXERCISES.

Each unit offers a variety of post-reading exercises. Both the choice and the use of the exercises are flexible and will depend on the individual teaching environment and style. The exercises might be used for pair or small-group work, or for programmed instruction, with the teacher selecting exercises to match the needs of particular students. The exercises can also be used in a teacher-centered classroom. The vocabulary and comprehension exercises can be completed orally or in writing. The perforated answer key at the back of the book affords the teacher a choice in the method of correcting the exercises. Students can work independently, in pairs, or in small groups, verifying their answers against those in the answer key. Or the instructor can lead the students in answering the questions. The exercises could also be assigned as homework.

Vocabulary. The vocabulary exercises are designed to aid comprehension by helping define unfamiliar words. Some of the exercises encourage guessing meaning through context clues; others introduce paraphrasing; still others ask students to guess meaning by answering "or" questions based on the text. All the exercises try to discourage students from relying on bilingual dictionaries. Students should rely instead on pictures, titles, context clues, and other sources to discover meaning.

Comprehension. The comprehension exercises are not intended to test the students' understanding of the reading as much as to introduce reading skills that will foster comprehension while helping to clarify meaning.

Understanding the Main Idea is a multiple-choice exercise. It asks the students to look at the main ideas in the readings.

Understanding Details recycles some of the vocabulary from the vocabulary exercises, verifies comprehension, and encourages the development of scanning techniques. The latter can be further exploited by having students scan for self-correction.

Understanding Pronouns are exercises in identifying pronoun referents. Pronouns relate sentences of a text to each other and enrich the texture of a written passage by eliminating the need to repeat nouns. The pronoun exercises are seen not as grammar exercises, but as a tool to aid comprehension and illustrate paragraph cohesion.

Finding Information asks the students to scan for answers to specific questions about the reading.

Understanding Cause and Effect, Reasons, and *Time Relationships* focus the students' attention on relationships expressed by the words *because, so, to* (meaning "in order to"), and *when*.

Making Inferences helps students interpret underlying meaning in the text. These exercises ask students to judge the validity of statements based on their understanding of the reading, and to support their opinions with references to statements in the text.

Reviewing the Story offers an opportunity for students to retell the story. A modified cloze passage, this exercise recycles vocabulary, encourages recall of information, simplifies and abbreviates the story so that students can see the text in a new form, and practices scanning, asking the students to self-check by looking back at the story.

Discussion and Writing. Two spin-off exercises end each unit. A discussion exercise asks students to personalize the ideas and themes presented in each reading by discussing questions with classmates and by exchanging information about the culture, weather, and geography of their respective countries. It is hoped that these discussions will provide further pleasure from the reading process and give insights into cultural similarities and differences.

The final exercise is a guided writing based on the reading.

The exercises are not included to make the students struggle. The reading selections and exercises in MORE TRUE STORIES are intended to offer pleasure in reading by building the students' confidence along with their reading skills, and by stimulating their imagination and interest in things incredible but true.

MORE TRUE STORIES is preceded by TRUE STORIES IN THE NEWS, a beginning reader.

Contents

UNIT 1

1. PRE-READING

Look at the picture.

- What is the dog doing?
- Where is the dog going?

Puppy Love

"SHIRO! Shiro!"
Mr. and Mrs. Nakamura were worried. Their dog Shiro was missing. "Shiro!" They called again and again. Mr. and Mrs. Nakamura lived on a small island in Japan. They looked everywhere on the island, but they didn't find Shiro.

The next day Mr. Nakamura heard a noise at the front door. He opened the door, and there was Shiro. Shiro was very wet, and he was shivering.

A few days later Shiro disappeared again. He disappeared in the morning, and he came back late at night. When he came back, he was wet and shivering.

Shiro began to disappear often. He always disappeared in the morning and came back late at night. He was always wet when he came back.

Mr. Nakamura was curious. "Where does Shiro go?" he wondered. "Why is he wet when he comes back?"

One morning Mr. Nakamura followed Shiro. Shiro walked to the beach. He ran into the water and began to swim. Mr. Nakamura jumped into his boat and followed his dog. Shiro swam for about two miles.[1] Then he was tired, so he climbed onto a rock and rested. A few minutes later he jumped back into the water and continued swimming.

Shiro swam for three hours. Then he arrived at an island. He walked onto the beach, shook the water off, and walked toward town. Mr. Nakamura followed him. Shiro walked to a house. A dog was waiting in front of the house. Shiro ran to the dog, and the two dogs began to play. The dog's name was Marilyn. Marilyn was Shiro's girlfriend.

Marilyn lived on Zamami, another Japanese island. Shiro and the Nakamuras used to live on Zamami. Then, in the summer of 1986, they moved to Aka, a smaller island. Shiro missed Marilyn very much and wanted to be with her. But Shiro wanted to be with the Nakamuras, too. So, Shiro lived with the Nakamuras on the island of Aka and swam to Zamami to visit Marilyn.

People were amazed when they heard about Shiro. The distance from Aka to Zamami is two and a half miles.[2] The ocean between the islands is very rough. "Nobody can swim from Aka to Zamami!" the people said.

Shiro became famous. Many people went to Zamami because they wanted to see Shiro. During one Japanese holiday, 3,000 people visited Zamami. They waited on the beach for Shiro. "Maybe Shiro will swim to Zamami today," they said. They all wanted to see Shiro, the dog who was in love.

[1] 3.2 kilometers
[2] 4 kilometers

2. VOCABULARY

Complete the sentences. Find the right words. Circle the letter of your answer.

1. Shiro _____. Mr. and Mrs. Nakamura looked everywhere for him, but they couldn't find him. Their dog was missing.
   a. ate
   b. slept
   c. disappeared

2. Shiro always came back at night. He was wet and cold, so he was _____.
   a. shivering
   b. swimming
   c. playing

3. Mr. Nakamura asked, "Where does Shiro go?" Mr. Nakamura wanted to know. He was _____.
   a. tired
   b. busy
   c. curious

4. People said, "We can't swim from Aka to Zamami. But Shiro can!" People were _____ when they heard about Shiro.
   a. worried
   b. angry
   c. amazed

3. COMPREHENSION

UNDERSTANDING THE MAIN IDEA

Circle the letter of the best answer.

1. "Puppy Love" is about
   a. two islands in Japan.
   b. a Japanese holiday.
   c. a dog who visits his girlfriend.
2. People were amazed when they heard about Shiro because
   a. dogs don't usually fall in love.
   b. swimming from Aka to Zamami is very difficult.
   c. "Shiro" is an unusual name for a dog.

UNDERSTANDING CAUSE AND EFFECT

Find the best way to complete each sentence. Write the letter of your answer on the line.

1. _c_ Mr. and Mrs. Nakamura were worried

2. ____ Shiro was always wet when he came back

3. ____ Mr. Nakamura followed Shiro

4. ____ Shiro swam to Zamami

5. ____ Three thousand people went to Zamami

a. because his girlfriend lived there.

b. because he was curious.

c. because their dog was missing.

d. because he swam in the ocean.

e. because they wanted to see Shiro.

REVIEWING THE STORY

Do you remember the story? Complete each sentence. Then read the story again. Were you right?

Mr. Nakamura was curious about his dog Shiro. Shiro often ____disappeared____ in the morning and _____ back late at night. He _____ always wet when he came back.
    One morning Mr. Nakamura _____ Shiro. Shiro walked to the beach, ran into the water, and began to _____ . Shiro swam for about two miles. Then he was tired, so he climbed onto a rock and _____ . A few minutes later he continued

swimming. He swam to Zamami, a Japanese _____ .
7

Marilyn lived on Zamami. Marilyn was Shiro's _____ .
8

People were amazed when they heard _____ Shiro.
9

The _____ from Aka to Zamami is two and a half miles.
10

The ocean between the islands is very _____ .
11

Shiro became _____ . Many people went to Zamami
12

because they wanted to see Shiro, the dog who was in

_____ .
13

---

4. DISCUSSION

Think about these questions. Discuss your answers with your classmates.

1. Shiro was famous in Japan. Are any animals famous in your country?
2. Which animals are popular pets in your country?
3. In the United States many people keep their dogs and cats in the house. Some pets sleep in the bedroom and eat in the kitchen. Where do people in your country keep their pets?
4. Which animals do you like? Which animals do you dislike?
5. Has an animal ever hurt you or scared you? What happened?

---

5. WRITING

Find a classmate who has a pet. Ask your classmate these questions.

1. What kind of pet do you have?
2. What is your pet's name?
3. How old is your pet?
4. Is your pet smart like Shiro?
5. Does your pet do anything unusual?
6. Do you enjoy your pet?

You can write a paragraph from your classmate's answers. Here is an example.

Irma has a pet goldfish. His name is Tiger, and he is about one year old. Irma named her goldfish Tiger because he has stripes like a Tiger. Tiger is not smart like Shiro. Tiger doesn't do anything unusual. He just swims around in his goldfish bowl. Irma enjoys Tiger, but she doesn't like to change the water in Tiger's bowl.

Now write your paragraph.

1. PRE-READING

Look at the picture.

- Who are these people?
- Why is the woman holding flowers?
- What is the man doing?
- Why is he doing that?

Surprise! It's Your Wedding!

"**G**OODNIGHT, John."

"Goodnight, Lynn."

Lynn Millington kissed her boyfriend goodnight. He walked to his car and drove away. Lynn walked into her house. It was midnight. Her parents were sleeping, and the house was quiet. Lynn sat down on the sofa. She had a problem, and she needed some time to think.

Lynn's boyfriend was John Biggin. John loved Lynn, and Lynn loved John. They were very happy together. What was the problem? Lynn wanted to get married. John wanted to get married, too. But John was afraid.

Sometimes Lynn and John talked about getting married. "Let's get married in June," Lynn said. "June is a beautiful month for a wedding."

"June?" John asked. "This June? Let's not get married in June. Let's wait a little longer."

Lynn waited . . . and waited. She was very patient. She was patient, but she wanted to get married. Lynn's parents liked John, and John's parents liked Lynn. Their parents wanted them to get married, too. Suddenly Lynn had an idea. "John's parents will help me!" she thought.

The next morning Lynn telephoned John's parents. "I need your help," Lynn told them. "John wants to get married, but he's afraid. Let's plan a wedding for John and me. It will be this Saturday. Invite your family. But don't tell John about the wedding."

Next, Lynn telephoned Bob Raper. Bob was John's best friend. "I need your help," Lynn told Bob. "Tell John that you're getting married this Saturday. Invite him to your wedding."

Bob wasn't really getting married on Saturday. It was a trick. John and Lynn were getting married on Saturday, but John didn't know it.

On Saturday morning John put on his best suit. Then he drove to the courthouse in Bridlington, England. He walked into the courthouse and looked around. He saw his friend Bob. He saw his girlfriend, Lynn. Then he saw his parents, relatives, and friends. He saw Lynn's family and friends. Suddenly John understood. This was not Bob's wedding! This was John's wedding! John began to shake, but he didn't run away. Twenty minutes later John and Lynn were husband and wife.

After the wedding a photographer took pictures of John and Lynn. In one picture John is pretending to punch Lynn. He is pretending that he is angry. John is not really angry. He is smiling. Lynn, of course, is smiling, too.

---

2. VOCABULARY

Complete the sentences. Find the right words. Circle the letter of your answer.

1. John and Lynn got married. After the _____ a photographer took pictures.
   a. class
   b. wedding
   c. coffee break

2. Lynn waited and waited. She was very _____.
   a. patient
   b. old
   c. famous

3. Bob told John, "I'm getting married on Saturday." Bob wasn't really getting married on Saturday. It was _____.
   a. an accident
   b. a problem
   c. a trick

4. In the picture John is pretending that he is _____ Lynn.
   a. kissing
   b. following
   c. punching

3. COMPREHENSION

UNDERSTANDING THE MAIN IDEA

Circle the letter of the best answer.

1. What was Lynn's problem?
   a. John's parents didn't like her.
   b. Lynn loved John's best friend.
   c. Lynn wanted to get married, but John was afraid.

2. John and Lynn's wedding was unusual because
   a. Lynn didn't wear a white dress.
   b. John didn't know about the wedding.
   c. the wedding was at a courthouse.

UNDERSTANDING DETAILS

Read the sentences. One word in each sentence is not correct. Find the word and cross it out. Write the correct word.

1. John loved Lynn and wanted to get married, but he was ~~angry.~~ *afraid*

2. Lynn told John's parents, "I need your money."

3. "Let's plan a party for John and me," Lynn told John's parents.

4. Next, Lynn telephoned Bob Raper, who was John's boss.

5. She told him, "Tell John that you're getting angry, and invite him to the wedding."

6. Bob wasn't really getting married; it was a problem.

7. On Saturday morning John put on his best suit and drove to the hospital in Bridlington, England.

8. At the courthouse he telephoned Lynn, his friends, and his relatives.

9. Suddenly he understood: this was Bob's wedding!

10. Twenty minutes later John and Lynn were boyfriend and wife.

UNDERSTANDING CAUSE AND EFFECT

Find the best way to complete each sentence. Write the letter of your answer on the line.

1. _b_ Lynn needed some time to think, so

2. ____ Lynn was very patient, so

3. ____ Lynn needed help, so

4. ____ The wedding was a surprise, so

a. she waited and waited.

b. she sat down on the sofa.

c. nobody told John about the wedding.

d. she telephoned John's parents.

4. DISCUSSION

Think about these questions. Discuss your answers with your classmates.

1. In the picture John is smiling. Is he happy that he is married? What do you think?
2. Lynn planned the wedding, but she didn't tell John. The wedding was a surprise for him. Was that a good idea or a bad idea?
3. John didn't want to get married because he was afraid. Why do you think John was afraid? Are you (or were you) afraid to get married? Why or why not?
4. In many countries, a man asks a woman, "Will you marry me?" If the woman says "Yes," they get married. What is the custom in your country?

5. WRITING

Is it better to be married or single? Fill in the chart below. Then discuss your answers with your classmates.

It is better to be married. Why?	It is better to be single. Why?
1. _____ _____	1. _____ _____
2. _____ _____	2. _____ _____
3. _____ _____	3. _____ _____

UNIT 3

1. PRE-READING

Look at the pictures.

- How old is the boy?
- How old is the girl?
- Why is she holding toys and balloons?

The Gift

DONNA Ashlock, a 14-year-old girl from California, was very sick. She had a bad heart. "Donna needs a new heart," her doctors said. "She must have a new heart, or she will die soon."

Felipe Garza, 15, was worried about Donna. Felipe was Donna's friend. He liked Donna very much. He liked her freckles, and he liked her smile. Felipe didn't want Donna to die.

Felipe talked to his mother about Donna. "I'm going to die," Felipe told his mother, "and I'm going to give my heart to Donna."

Felipe's mother didn't pay much attention to Felipe. "Felipe is just kidding," she thought. "Felipe is not going to die. He's strong and healthy."

But Felipe was not healthy. He had terrible headaches sometimes. "My head really hurts," he often told his friends. Felipe never told his parents about his headaches.

One morning Felipe woke up with a sharp pain in his head. He was dizzy, and he couldn't breathe. The Garzas rushed Felipe to the hospital. Doctors at the hospital had terrible news for the Garzas. "Felipe's brain is dead," the doctors said. "We can't save him."

The Garzas were very sad. But they remembered Felipe's words. "Felipe wanted to give his heart to Donna," they told the doctors.

The doctors did several tests. Then they told the Garzas, "We can give Felipe's heart to Donna."

On January 5, 1986, doctors took out Felipe's heart and rushed the heart to Donna. Doctors took out Donna's heart. Then they put Felipe's heart in Donna's chest. In a short time the heart began to beat.

The operation was a success. Felipe's heart was beating in Donna's chest. But Donna didn't know it. Her parents and doctors didn't tell her. They waited until she was stronger. Then they told her about Felipe. "I feel very sad," Donna said, "but I'm thankful to Felipe."

Three months after the operation, Donna Ashlock went back to school. She has to have regular checkups, and she has to take medicine every day. But she is living a normal life.

Felipe's brother John says, "Every time we see Donna, we think of Felipe. She has Felipe's heart in her. That gives us great peace."

2. VOCABULARY

Which sentences have the same meaning as the sentences in the story? Circle the letter of the correct answer.

1. Felipe's mother didn't *pay* much *attention* to Felipe. "Felipe is just *kidding*," she thought.

   a. Felipe's mother didn't give him any money. "He's only a child," she thought.

   b. Felipe's mother didn't listen carefully to Felipe. "He's not serious," she thought.

2. Felipe woke up with a *sharp pain* in his head, and he was *dizzy*.

   a. Felipe's head hurt very much, and he thought, "The room is going around and around."

   b. Felipe's head hurt a little, and he thought, "I was having a wonderful dream."

3. Felipe couldn't *breathe*.

   a. Felipe couldn't get air.

   b. Felipe couldn't eat.

4. Donna is living a normal life, but she has to have regular *checkups*.

   a. Donna is healthy now, but she has to pay the doctor. She pays by check.

   b. Donna is healthy now, but she goes to the doctor sometimes. The doctor checks and makes sure her heart is working well.

3. COMPREHENSION

UNDERSTANDING THE MAIN IDEA

Circle the letter of the best answer.

1. The title of the story is "The Gift." What was the gift?
   - **a.** the toys and balloons in the picture
   - **b.** Felipe's heart
   - **c.** the operation

2. Why did Donna feel sad and thankful?
   - **a.** She had an operation, but she went back to school three months later.
   - **b.** She has to take medicine every day, but she is living a normal life.
   - **c.** Her friend Felipe died, but he gave Donna his heart.

UNDERSTANDING CAUSE AND EFFECT

Find the best way to complete each sentence. Write the letter of your answer on the line.

1. _b_ Felipe Garza was worried about Donna

2. ___ Felipe's mother didn't pay much attention to Felipe

3. ___ Donna's parents didn't tell her that Felipe had died

4. ___ Donna Ashlock is alive today

- **a.** because Felipe Garza gave her his heart.
- **b.** because she was very sick.
- **c.** because they wanted to wait until she was stronger.
- **d.** because she thought Felipe was just kidding.

UNDERSTANDING PRONOUNS

Look at the pronouns. What do they mean? Write the letter of your answer on the line.

1. _d_ *They* said Donna needed a new heart.

2. ___ *He* was Donna's friend.

3. ___ Felipe told *them* his head hurt.

4. ___ *It* was a success.

5. ___ Donna has to take *it* every day.

- **a.** Felipe Garza
- **b.** Felipe's friends
- **c.** medicine
- **d.** doctors
- **e.** Donna's operation

4. DISCUSSION

Think about these questions. Discuss your answers with your classmates.

1. The doctors put Felipe's heart in Donna's chest. Donna had a heart transplant. Do doctors in your country do heart transplants? Do they do other kinds of transplants?
2. Donna's operation was in a hospital in San Francisco, California. Have you ever been in a hospital? Why were you there?

5. WRITING

The title of the story is "The Gift." Would you like a gift? Imagine this: One day you come home from English class and walk into the kitchen. A big box is on the kitchen table. The box has your name on it. It's a gift for you! You open the box and look at your gift. It is something you have wanted for a long time. What is your gift? Write about it. Here is an example.

When I walked into the kitchen, I smelled something delicious. It smelled like food from my country. "That's impossible!" I thought. Then I saw the box and opened it. Inside the box was a dinner with my favorite foods. My mother sent the dinner from Panama! The dinner was rice, beans, and ceviche. (Ceviche is seafood with lemon, garlic, and onions; it is very spicy.) I ate the dinner. It was delicious. Thank you, Mom!

1. PRE-READING

Look at the picture.

- How old is the boy?
- What is he doing?

Oh Boy, What a Ride!

ROBERT Vogel is a police officer in Rye, New York. One morning Officer Vogel was drinking coffee in a restaurant. He was on his coffee break. Suddenly the doors of the restaurant opened, and a man ran in. "Officer!" the man yelled. "A car is going down the street—and a little kid is driving it!"

Officer Vogel ran out of the restaurant. He saw a station wagon. It was going slowly—about 25 miles[1] an hour—but it wasn't going very straight. He jumped into his police car and followed the station wagon. When he was behind it, he turned on his red light and siren. The station wagon moved to the side of the road and stopped.

Officer Vogel got out of his police car, hurried to the station wagon, and looked inside. The driver was a little boy. His name was Rocco Morabito, and he was five years old. In the back seat was Rocco's little sister. She was only two years old. Both children were crying.

"I want my Mommy!" Rocco cried. "But she can't get here. I have the car." Then Rocco had an idea. "Just a minute," he told Officer Vogel. "I can drive. I'll go get her."

"No!" Officer Vogel said. "You stay with me!"

Officer Vogel drove Rocco and his sister to the police station. Then he called their mother. Officer Vogel and Rocco's mother had a lot of questions for Rocco. Their first question was: "Where did you get the car keys?"

Rocco said, "From the top of the refrigerator." At seven o'clock that morning Rocco's father was at work and his mother was sleeping. Rocco saw the car keys on top of the refrigerator. He pulled a chair over to the refrigerator, climbed up on the chair, and took the keys.

Rocco went to the garage and got into the car. Then he started the engine. When Rocco's sister heard the engine, she ran to the car and began to cry. She wanted to go with him, so Rocco opened the back door and let her in the car.

Rocco backed the car out of the garage and drove away. It was 7 A.M.—rush hour—so there was a lot of traffic. Rocco drove one mile[2] in heavy traffic. Then Officer Vogel stopped him.

Newspapers and TV stations heard about Rocco, and a lot of reporters went to his house. One reporter asked Rocco, "What do you want to be when you grow up?"

Rocco smiled. "I want to be a truck driver," he said.

[1]40 kilometers
[2]1.6 kilometers

---

2. VOCABULARY

Think about the story and answer the questions.

1. A man ran into the restaurant. "Officer!" the man *yelled*. Did the man speak loudly or quietly?
2. Officer Vogel jumped into his police car. When he was behind the station wagon, he turned on the *siren*. Rocco heard the siren and stopped. Does a siren make a very quiet sound or a very loud sound?
3. Rocco's sister wanted to go with him, so Rocco opened the back door and *let* her *in* the car. Did Rocco's sister go with Rocco, or did she stay in the garage?
4. At 7 A.M.—*rush hour*—Rocco drove one mile in *heavy traffic*. Were there a lot of cars, or were there only a few cars?

3. COMPREHENSION

UNDERSTANDING THE MAIN IDEA

Circle the letter of the best answer.

1. This story is about
   a. a police officer.
   (b.) a little boy who drove a car.
   c. safe driving in New York.

2. The story has a happy ending because
   a. Rocco was a very good driver.
   b. Rocco didn't get hurt.
   c. Rocco wants to be a truck driver.

UNDERSTANDING DETAILS

Read the sentences. One word in each sentence is not correct. Find the word and cross it out. Write the correct word.

1. Robert Vogel is a *police officer* ~~salesman~~ in Rye, New York.

2. One morning he was drinking coffee in a library.

3. Suddenly the doors of the restaurant opened, and a woman ran in.

4. The man yelled, "A car is going down the street—and a little kid is fixing it!"

5. Officer Vogel jumped into his police car and hit the station wagon.

6. The driver's name was Rocco Morabito, and he was 50 years old.

7. Rocco took the car keys from the top of the television.

8. Rocco opened the back seat and let his sister in the car.

9. Rocco drove one mile in light traffic.

10. A lot of mechanics went to Rocco's house.

UNDERSTANDING REASONS

Find the best way to complete each sentence. Write the letter of your answer on the line.

1. _d_ Officer Vogel went to a restaurant
2. ____ Rocco climbed up on a chair
3. ____ Rocco opened the back door
4. ____ Officer Vogel called Rocco's mother
5. ____ Reporters went to Rocco's house

a. to get the car keys.
b. to ask him questions.
c. to let his sister in the car.
d. to drink a cup of coffee.
e. to tell her, "Your son is at the police station."

4. DISCUSSION

Think about these questions. Discuss your answers with your classmates.

1. Rocco drove his family's car. That was bad. Did you do anything bad when you were a child? Tell your classmates about it.
2. Rocco was only five years old, so he didn't have a driver's license. Do you have a driver's license? Was the driving test easy or difficult? Describe the test.
3. Rocco was too young to drive, so Officer Vogel took him to the police station. What happens in your country when someone:

   ■ drinks alcohol and drives a car?　■ throws trash out the car window?
   ■ drives too fast?　■ parks in a "NO PARKING" zone?
   ■ drives through a red light?

4. Has a police officer ever stopped you? Why did the police officer stop you? What happened?
5. Officer Vogel wanted to help Rocco. He was friendly. Are police officers usually friendly in your country?

5. WRITING

When Officer Vogel went back to the police station, he had to write a report. This is how he began his report:

At 7 a.m. I was drinking coffee at the Coffee Cup restaurant...

Finish Officer Vogel's report.

UNIT 5

1. PRE-READING

Look at the picture.

- Why are the two men standing together?
- Where are the men from?
- How old is the photograph?
- Who are the two young boys?

The Twins of Siam

A YOUNG mother was lying on a bed. She had just given birth to twin boys. She was tired but happy. A woman was helping her. Suddenly the woman screamed. "What's the matter?" the mother cried. She lifted her head and looked at her babies. The babies were joined at their chests. She could not separate them.

That happened in Siam—now called Thailand—in 1811. The mother named her babies Chang and Eng. Chang and Eng grew up and became the famous Siamese twins.

People came from all over Siam to stare at the twins. One day, when the twins were 18, an American saw them. He thought, "I can make money with the twins." He asked Chang and Eng, "Will you come with me to the United States?" Chang and Eng wanted to go to the United States, so they went with the man. They never saw Siam or their family again.

Chang and Eng traveled with the American for ten years. Later they traveled alone. People paid to see them and ask them questions about their lives. Finally, the twins got tired of traveling. They got tired of answering questions. They decided to live quietly in North Carolina.

Soon after they moved to North Carolina, the twins met two sisters. The sisters' names were Adelaide and Sarah. The twins fell in love with the sisters. Chang married Adelaide, and Eng married Sarah. The marriages were very unusual. Adelaide and Sarah lived in separate houses. The twins lived in one house for four days. Then they went to the other house for four days. The marriages were unusual, but they were long and happy. Chang and Adelaide had ten children, and Eng and Sarah had eleven children.

The twins were happy with Adelaide and Sarah, but they were not always happy with each other. Sometimes they argued, and they didn't talk to each other. They asked doctor after doctor, "Please separate us." Every doctor said, "I can't separate you. The operation is too dangerous." So, the twins stayed joined together.

One night, when the twins were 63, Eng suddenly woke up. He looked at Chang, who was lying beside him. Chang was not breathing. Eng screamed for help, and one of his sons came.

"Uncle Chang is dead," the young man said.

"Then I am going to die, too," Eng said, and he began to cry. Two hours later Eng was dead.

For 63 years the twins of Siam lived together as one. In the end, they also died as one.

2. VOCABULARY

Read the sentences. What is the meaning of the words in italics? Circle the letter of the right answer.

1. A woman was helping the young mother. Suddenly the woman *screamed*. "What's the matter?" the mother cried.
   a. cried in a loud voice
   b. smiled happily

2. The babies were joined at their chests. She could not *separate* them.
   a. take them apart
   b. wake them up

3. People came from all over Siam to *stare* at the twins.
   a. yell
   b. look

4. The twins were not always happy with each other. Sometimes they *argued*.
   a. spoke quietly
   b. spoke in angry voices

3. COMPREHENSION

UNDERSTANDING THE MAIN IDEA

Circle the letter of the best answer.

1. This story is about
   a. dangerous operations.
   b. unusual marriages.
   c. Siamese twin brothers.
2. The twins talked to many doctors because
   a. the twins were often sick.
   b. they wanted the doctors to separate them.
   c. the doctors wanted to study the twins.

UNDERSTANDING DETAILS

Read the sentences. One word in each sentence is not correct. Find the word and cross it out. Write the correct word.

1. The story happened in Siam — now called ~~China~~ *Thailand* — in 1811.

2. Chang and Eng grew up and became the famous Siamese doctors.

3. People came from all over Siam to laugh at the twins.

4. An Australian asked Chang and Eng to come to the United States.

5. Chang and Eng traveled with the American for ten days.

6. After they moved to North Carolina, the twins telephoned two sisters.

7. The marriages were unusual, but they were long and unhappy.

8. Every doctor said, "I can separate you because the operation is too dangerous."

UNDERSTANDING REASONS

Find the best way to complete each sentence. Write the letter of your answer on the line.

1. _____ The young mother lifted her head
2. _____ Chang and Eng went to the United States
3. _____ People paid
4. _____ The twins went to doctor after doctor

a. to ask the twins questions.
b. to ask about an operation.
c. to travel with the American.
d. to look at her babies.

4. DISCUSSION

Think about these questions. Discuss your answers with your classmates.

1. Are there any twins in your family? Tell your classmates about them.
2. Chang and Adelaide had ten children, and Eng and Sarah had eleven children. How many brothers and sisters do you have? How many brothers and sisters did your parents have? Do people in your country have big families?
3. Chang and Eng traveled for over ten years. Do you like to travel? Where would you like to go? Which places have you visited? Which was your favorite place? Think about something beautiful or interesting that you saw there. Tell your classmates about it.

5. WRITING

The twins married two sisters. Their marriages were happy. Not all marriages are happy every day. Look at the picture of a husband and wife. Why is the husband angry? What is he saying? Write it.

Look at the next picture. Why is the wife angry? What is she saying? Write it.

What did you write? Tell your classmates.

1. PRE-READING

Look at the picture.

- Who are the women?
- Why are they smiling?

The Baby Exchange

SELMA Scarausi looked at her baby daughter and smiled. The baby smiled back. Selma began to cry. "I love my baby very much," Selma thought. "But is she really my baby?"

Selma's baby was born in June 1985 at a hospital in São Paulo, Brazil. A few days later Selma and the baby came home from the hospital. Friends and relatives were surprised when they saw the baby. The baby didn't look like her parents. The baby had dark skin and curly hair. Selma and her husband had light skin and straight hair. "Babies change," everyone thought. "She will look like her parents when she is older."

But the baby didn't change. When she was nine months old, she still looked very different from her parents. Selma and her husband, Paulo, took the baby back to the hospital. "Are you sure this is our baby?" they asked the hospital director.

"Of course she is your baby," the director said. "Immediately after the babies are born, we give them bracelets with numbers. Your baby was number 51. You left the hospital with baby 51. A mistake is impossible."

"A mistake is possible," Selma and Paulo thought. "We have another family's baby. And somewhere another family has our baby. But São Paulo is a city of seven million people. How can we find our baby?"

Selma and Paulo went to the hospital again. A nurse at the hospital told Paulo, "I remember another couple. Their baby didn't look like them. The parents had dark skin, but the baby had light skin. The father had very curly hair, but the baby had straight hair." The nurse gave Paulo the couple's address.

The next day Selma took her baby to the couple's house. She knocked, and a woman opened the door. The woman took one look at Selma's baby and fainted. Selma helped her into the house. There, in the living room, was a nine-month-old baby. Selma knew that the baby was hers.

Selma and Paulo's baby was living with Maria and Luiz Souza. The Souzas also had wondered about their baby. She looked so different from them. When Maria Souza saw the baby in Selma's arms, she, too, knew the baby was hers.

The hospital made a mistake. Both babies were born at the hospital on the same day. The hospital gave both babies the number 51.

During the next weeks the two families prepared to exchange babies. First they exchanged information about the babies' habits. Then they exchanged toys and clothes. Finally, with smiles and tears, they exchanged babies.

2. VOCABULARY

Which words or picture has the same meaning as the words in the story? Circle the letter of the correct answer.

1. Immediately after the babies are born, we give them *bracelets* with numbers.

   a.   b.
   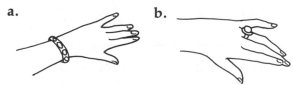

2. Maria Souza took one look at Selma's baby and *fainted*.

   a. left the house with the baby

   b. fell to the floor and didn't move

3. The two families exchanged information about the babies' *habits*.

   a. things people do every day

   b. places people like to go

4. Finally, with smiles and *tears*, they exchanged babies.

   a. water that comes from people's eyes when they cry

   b. gifts that people give to babies

3. COMPREHENSION

UNDERSTANDING THE MAIN IDEA

Circle the letter of the best answer.

1. The story is about
   a. the city of São Paulo, Brazil.
   b. a couple who got the wrong baby.
   c. babies' habits, toys, and clothes.
2. Selma and Paulo thought, "We have the wrong baby" because
   a. hospitals sometimes make mistakes.
   b. they wanted a son, not a daughter.
   c. their baby didn't look like them.

FINDING INFORMATION

Read the questions. Find the answers in the story. Write the answers.

1. Do the Scarausis live in Brazil or in China?

   They live in Brazil.

2. Did Selma have a baby girl or a baby boy?

   _____

3. Did the baby get a toy or a number at the hospital?

   _____

4. Did Selma and Paulo take their baby back to the hospital or back to the school?

   _____

5. Is São Paulo a city of seven million people or seven thousand people?

   _____

6. Did the nurse give Paulo the couple's baby or the couple's address?

   _____

7. Who made a mistake—the hospital or the Scarausis?

   _____

UNDERSTANDING CAUSE AND EFFECT

Find the best way to complete each sentence. Write the letter of your answer on the line.

1. _____ Friends and relatives were surprised

2. _____ Selma and Paulo went back to the hospital

3. _____ The hospital director said that a mistake was impossible

4. _____ It was difficult for Selma and Paulo to find their baby

5. _____ Maria Souza fainted

a. because São Paulo is a big city.

b. because she knew that the baby in Selma's arms was her baby.

c. because they thought they had the wrong baby.

d. because the hospital gave each baby a number.

e. because the baby didn't look like her parents.

4. DISCUSSION

Think about these questions. Discuss your answers with your classmates.

1. Selma and Paulo's baby didn't look like them. Do you look like your parents? Do you look more like your mother or more like your father? Do you look like your sisters and brothers?

2. Selma and Paulo named their baby Aline. The Souzas named their baby Ariane. In the United States some popular names for baby girls are Jennifer, Jessica, Sarah, Melissa, and Nicole. Popular names for baby boys are Michael, Jason, Matthew, Christopher, and David. What are some popular names for babies in your country? Is your name popular?

5. WRITING

The families exchanged information about the babies' habits. What are your habits? What do you do every day? Do you drink coffee every morning? Do you exercise every day?

Make a list of some of your habits.

1. _____

2. _____

3. _____

4. _____

UNIT 7

1. PRE-READING

Look at the picture.

■ What is the man doing?

Why Can't They Quit?

THE man in the picture is Ali. Ali is from Saudi Arabia, but he is living in the United States. Ali will stay in the United States for one year. During the year, Ali wants to do two things. First, he wants to learn English. Second, he wants to quit smoking.

Ali has smoked for nine years. He smokes a pack of cigarettes every day. Ali says, "I tried to quit smoking in Saudi Arabia, but it was impossible. My brothers smoke. My friends smoke. At parties and at meetings, almost all the men smoke. Here in the United States not as many people smoke. I think that in the United States I can stop smoking. It will be easier to quit here."

Many smokers are like Ali. They want to quit smoking. They know that smoking is bad for their health. They know that it can cause cancer and heart disease. But it is difficult for them to stop smoking. It is difficult because cigarettes have a drug in them. The drug is nicotine. People who smoke a lot need nicotine.

The first few times a person smokes, the smoker usually feels terrible. The nicotine makes the person sick. In a few days, the smoker's body gets used to the nicotine, and the smoker feels fine. Later, the smoker needs nicotine to feel fine. Without it, the smoker feels terrible. The smoker is addicted to nicotine.

What happens when people quit smoking? What happens when smokers don't have nicotine? People who quit smoking are often depressed and nervous for weeks. Some people want to eat sweets, so they gain weight.

Doctors sometimes give special chewing gum to people who want to quit smoking. The chewing gum has a little nicotine in it. When smokers need nicotine, they don't smoke cigarettes. They chew the gum instead. Each day the smokers try to chew the gum less often. With the gum, people can quit smoking and then gradually give up nicotine.

It is very difficult to stop smoking. Many people who quit smoking will smoke again. At a party or maybe at work they will decide to smoke "just one" cigarette. Then they will smoke another cigarette, and another. Soon they are smokers again. Maybe there is only one easy way to quit smoking: never start.

2. VOCABULARY

Complete the sentences. Find the right words. Circle the letter of your answer.

1. Ali doesn't want to smoke. He wants to _____ smoking.
   a. try
   b. study
   c. quit

2. Smoking can _____ cancer and heart disease.
   a. cause
   b. help
   c. separate

3. When a person smokes for the first time, the nicotine makes the smoker sick. In a few days the smoker feels fine. The smoker's body _____ the nicotine.
   a. gets tired of
   b. gets used to
   c. gets angry at

4. People who smoke a lot need nicotine. They are _____ nicotine.
   a. addicted to
   b. afraid of
   c. worried about

3. COMPREHENSION

UNDERSTANDING THE MAIN IDEA

Circle the letter of the best answer.

1. It is difficult to quit smoking because
    a. a lot of people smoke at parties and meetings.
    b. many people who quit will smoke again.
    c. smokers are addicted to nicotine.
2. Nicotine is
    a. a kind of chewing gum.
    b. a drug in cigarettes.
    c. a sweet food.

UNDERSTANDING TIME RELATIONSHIPS

Find the best way to complete each sentence. Write the letter of your answer on the line.

1. ____ When people smoke for the first time,
2. ____ When people smoke for a long time,
3. ____ When smokers stop smoking,
4. ____ When people eat a lot of sweets

a. the nicotine usually makes them sick.
b. they are often depressed and nervous.
c. they become addicted to nicotine.
d. they usually gain weight.

REVIEWING THE STORY

Do you remember the story? Complete each sentence. Then read the story again. Were you right?

It is difficult to quit smoking because smokers are ___*addicted*___

to nicotine. Nicotine is a _____ . that is in cigarettes.

People who quit _____ are often depressed and

nervous. Some people _____ weight because they eat

sweets instead of smoking.

People who want to quit smoking sometimes chew a special

_____ . The gum has a _____ nicotine

in it. When smokers need nicotine, they _____ the gum.

It is very difficult _____ quit smoking, and many
                              8
people who quit will _____ again. Maybe there is only
                              9
one easy _____ to quit smoking: never start.
                   10

---

4. DISCUSSION

Think about these questions. Discuss your answers with your classmates.

1. Do you smoke? Do many men in your country smoke? Do many women in your country smoke?
2. In the United States cigarette companies advertise in magazines and newspapers, but not on TV or on the radio. Where do cigarette companies advertise in your country?
3. In the United States every pack of cigarettes and every cigarette ad has a warning. The warning says: "Cigarettes are dangerous. They are bad for your health." Do you think the warning stops people from smoking? What stops people from smoking?
4. Many people think that smoking is a bad habit. There are other bad habits. Some people, for example, drink too much coffee. Some people watch too much TV. Do you have any bad habits?

---

5. WRITING

Write about Ali.

1. *Ali is from Saudi Arabia.*
2. _____
3. _____
4. _____

Write about nicotine.

1. _____
2. _____
3. _____
4. _____

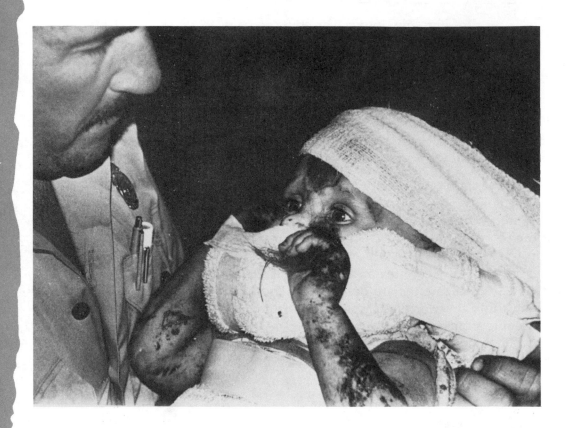

1. PRE-READING

Look at the picture.

- Why is the man holding the little girl?
- What happened to her?

Everybody's Baby

AT a day care center in Texas, children were playing outside. One of the children was Jessica McClure. She was 18 months old. Jessica's mother, who worked at the day care center, was watching the children. Suddenly Jessica fell and disappeared. Jessica's mother screamed and ran to her.

A well was in the yard of the day care center. The well was only eight inches across, and a rock always covered it. But children had moved the rock. When Jessica fell, she fell right into the well.

Jessica's mother reached inside the well, but she couldn't feel Jessica. She ran to a phone and dialed 911 for help.

Men from the fire department arrived. They discovered that Jessica was about 20 feet[1] down in the well. For the next hour the men talked and planned Jessica's rescue. Then they told Jessica's parents their plan.

"We can't go down into the well," they said. "It's too narrow. So, we're going to drill a hole next to the well. We'll drill down about 20 feet. Then we'll drill a tunnel across to Jessica. When we reach her, we'll bring her through the tunnel. Then we'll bring her up through our hole."

The men began to drill the hole at 11 A.M. on Wednesday, October 14, 1987. The men had a difficult job; they were drilling through solid rock. Two days later, on Friday morning, the men were still drilling. And Jessica McClure was still in the well.

During her days in the well, Jessica sometimes called for her mother. Sometimes she slept, sometimes she cried, and sometimes she sang.

All over the world, people waited for news of Jessica. They read about her in newspapers and watched her rescue on TV. Everyone worried about the little girl in the well.

At 8 P.M. on Friday, October 16, men reached Jessica and brought her up from the well. Then paramedics rushed her to the hospital. Jessica was dirty, hungry, thirsty, and tired. Her foot and forehead were badly injured. But Jessica was alive. A doctor at the hospital said, "Jessica is lucky she's very young. She's not going to remember this very well."

Maybe Jessica will not remember her days in the well. But her parents, her rescuers, and many other people around the world will not forget them.

After Jessica's rescue, one of the rescuers made a metal cover for the well. On the cover he wrote, "To Jessica, with love from all of us."

[1] 6 meters

2. VOCABULARY

Which words have the same meaning as the words in the story? Circle the letter of the correct answer.

1. The men said, "We can't go down into the well. It's only eight inches across. It's too *narrow*."

   a. big

   b. small

2. The men said, "We're going to *drill* a hole next to the well."

   a. make

   b. look at

3. Jessica had to go to the hospital because her foot and forehead were *injured*.

   a. small

   b. hurt

4. Jessica's *rescuers* will not forget her days in the well.

   a. the children who played with Jessica

   b. the men who saved Jessica

3. COMPREHENSION

UNDERSTANDING THE MAIN IDEA

Circle the letter of the best answer.

1. This story is about
   a. day care centers in Texas.
   b. the rescue of a little girl.
   c. drilling wells.
2. The story has a happy ending because
   a. Jessica was very young.
   b. Jessica was in the well only two days.
   c. the men rescued Jessica.

UNDERSTANDING DETAILS

Read the sentences. One word in each sentence is not correct. Find the word and cross it out. Write the correct word.

1. Jessica McClure was 18 ~~years~~ *months* old.

2. A well was in the kitchen of the day care center.

3. When Jessica fell, she fell right into the water.

4. Jessica's mother ran to a phone and wrote 911.

5. The men said, "We're going to drill a cover next to the well."

6. The men had a difficult job; they were drilling through soft rock.

7. At 8 P.M. on Friday, men reached Jessica and brought her down from the well.

8. Then paramedics rushed her to the restaurant.

9. A doctor at the hospital said, "Jessica is lucky she's very old."

10. After Jessica's rescue, a worker made a metal rock for the well.

UNDERSTANDING TIME RELATIONSHIPS

Find the best way to complete each sentence. Write the letter of your answer on the line.

1. _____ When Jessica fell,

2. _____ When Jessica's mother reached inside the well,

3. _____ When the men from the fire department arrived,

4. _____ When Jessica was in the well,

5. _____ When the rescuers reached Jessica,

a. she slept, cried, and sang.

b. they brought her through the tunnel and then up through their hole.

c. she couldn't feel Jessica.

d. she fell right into the well.

e. they discovered that Jessica was about 20 feet down in the well.

4. DISCUSSION

Think about these questions. Discuss your answers with your classmates.

1. Did you watch Jessica's rescue on TV or read about it in the newspaper? How did you feel?
2. Jessica's mother dialed 911. What number do you dial when
   - there is a fire?
   - you need an ambulance?
   - you need the police?
3. Have you ever rescued anybody? Have you ever seen a rescue? Tell your classmates about it.

5. WRITING

Read this story. It is in the present. Write the story again in the past.

Jessica is playing at a day care center. Suddenly she falls into a well. She falls about 20 feet and can't get out of the well.

Men from the fire department come. They can't go down into the well because it is too narrow. The men decide to drill a hole next to the well.

For the next 58 hours, the men drill the hole. Their job is very difficult because they are drilling through solid rock. Finally, they reach Jessica and bring her up from the well. Jessica's foot and forehead are badly injured, but she is alive. Everyone is very happy.

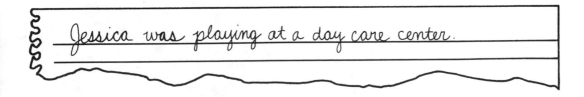

Jessica was playing at a day care center.

1. PRE-READING

Look at the picture.

- Where are these people?
- What is the man doing?

Please Pass the Bird Brains

DO you have a headache? Take an aspirin—or eat bird brains. Do you want beautiful skin? Use skin cream—or eat pearls. Is your hair turning gray? Color your hair—or eat black rice.

"Eat bird brains, pearls, and black rice?" some people ask. "How strange!" But for many Chinese people, bird brains, pearls, and black rice are not strange things to eat; they are good things to eat. They are good medicines, too.

Many Chinese believe that food can be medicine. They believe that eating bird brains, for example, stops headaches, soup with ground pearls is good for the skin, and black rice stops hair from turning gray.

Food that people use for medicine is called medicinal food. The Chinese have eaten medicinal food and spices for centuries. Ginger, for example, is a common spice in Chinese cooking. Ginger gives food a nice flavor. The Chinese began to use ginger many years ago. They used ginger not because it tasted good. They used ginger because it was medicinal. Ginger, they thought, was good for the digestion. It also helped people who had colds.

Pepper and garlic, too, were probably medicines a long time ago.

Some people don't believe that food and spices are good medicines. They want to buy their medicine in drugstores, not in supermarkets. Other people want to try medicinal food. They say, "Maybe medicinal food can't help me. But it can't hurt me, either."

People can try medicinal food at a Chinese restaurant in San Francisco, California. The restaurant serves medicinal food. The menus at the restaurant have a list of dinners. Next to each dinner there is information about the food. The information helps people order. "Queen's Secret," for example, is one dinner at the restaurant. This dinner has meat from chickens with black feathers. It is for women who want to look young.

A store is next to the restaurant. The store sells medicinal food. People who want to cook medicinal food at home can shop at the store. Alan Lau is the owner of both the restaurant and the store. In the picture he is working at the store. He is weighing something for a customer. Is it a spice? Is it medicine? Or is it both?

2. VOCABULARY

Think about the story and answer the questions.

1. Soup with *ground* pearls is good for the skin. Does the soup have very big pieces of pearls or very small pieces of pearls?
2. Chinese people have eaten medicinal food for *centuries*. Have the Chinese eaten medicinal food for hundreds of years or for only a few years?
3. Ginger is a *common* spice in Chinese cooking. Do the Chinese use ginger often or not very often?
4. Ginger is good for the *digestion*. Does ginger help the heart or the stomach?

3. COMPREHENSION

UNDERSTANDING THE MAIN IDEA

Circle the letter of the best answer.

1. "Please Pass the Bird Brains" is about
   a. eating bird brains.
   b. Chinese medicinal food.
   c. a Chinese restaurant.
2. People who like medicinal food say,
   a. "Food and spices can be good medicine."
   b. "I buy medicine only in drugstores."
   c. "Eating bird brains is strange."

UNDERSTANDING DETAILS

Read the sentences. One word in each sentence is not correct. Find the word and cross it out. Write the correct word.

1. Many Chinese people believe that ~~furniture~~ *food* can be medicine.

2. Eating bird brains stops backaches.

3. Soup with ground beef is good for the skin.

4. Black rice stops hair from turning red.

5. Food that is medicine is called delicious food.

6. The Chinese have eaten medicinal food for months.

7. Ginger, pepper, and garlic were medicines a short time ago.

8. People can try medicinal food at a bakery in San Francisco.

UNDERSTANDING PRONOUNS

Look at the pronouns. What do they mean? Write the letter of your answer on the line.

1. _____ *They* have used medicinal food for centuries.

2. _____ *It* is a common spice in Chinese cooking.

3. _____ *It* serves medicinal food.

4. _____ *It* is for women who want to look young.

a. ginger

b. a restaurant in California

c. meat from chickens with black feathers

d. the Chinese

4. DISCUSSION

People everywhere use medicinal food. They also use home remedies. For example, when someone has an earache, people in Italy put a little warm olive oil in the ear. Putting olive oil in the ear is a home remedy for an earache. Do your classmates use medicinal food and home remedies? Ask a classmate the questions below.

What does your family do when someone has:
- an earache?
- a cold?
- a sore throat?
- a headache?
- a stomachache?
- a burn?
- hiccups?
- a fever?

Share information about medicinal food and home remedies with the class.

5. WRITING

Imagine that there is a special medicinal food. It is not for headaches or stomachaches. This medicinal food is for problems. When you eat it, your problems go away.

You went to the store, bought the medicinal food, and ate it. Which problems went away? Write about them.

Here is an example.

I had three problems. My English was not good. I didn't have enough money. I didn't have a boyfriend. Then I ate the medicinal food. Now my English is perfect. I got a new job, and I make $50,000 a year. I have plenty of money. I also have a boyfriend. He is very handsome. That medicinal food was great!

UNIT 10

1. PRE-READING

Look at the picture.

- What are the women doing?
- Are the women doing anything unusual?

Margaret Patrick . . . Meet Ruth Eisenberg

RUTH Eisenberg and Margaret Patrick play the piano. They give concerts in the United States and in Canada, and they are often on TV. They are famous.

Why are these women famous? They play the piano well, but they are not famous because they play well. They are famous because Mrs. Eisenberg plays the piano with only her right hand, and Mrs. Patrick plays the piano with only her left hand. They sit next to each other and play the piano together. Mrs. Eisenberg plays one part of the music, and Mrs. Patrick plays the other part.

Both Mrs. Eisenberg and Mrs. Patrick love the piano. Mrs. Patrick was a piano teacher. She taught hundreds of students. She taught her own children, too. Then, when she was 69 years old, Mrs. Patrick had a stroke. She couldn't move or speak. Gradually she got better, but her right side was still very weak. She couldn't play the piano anymore. She was very sad.

Playing the piano was Mrs. Eisenberg's hobby. She often played five or six hours a day. Then, when she was 80 years old, she, too, had a stroke. She couldn't move the left side of her body. She couldn't play the piano anymore. She was very sad.

A few months after her stroke, Mrs. Eisenberg went to a senior citizens' center. A few weeks later, Mrs. Patrick went to the same center. The director was showing her around the center when Mrs. Patrick saw a piano. She looked sadly at the piano. "Is anything wrong?" the director asked. "No," Mrs. Patrick answered. "The piano brings back memories. Before my stroke, I played the piano." The director looked at Mrs. Patrick's weak right hand and said, "Wait here. I'll be right back." A few minutes later, the director came back with Mrs. Eisenberg. "Margaret Patrick," the director said, "meet Ruth Eisenberg. Before her stroke, she played the piano, too. She has a good right hand, and you have a good left hand. I think you two can do something wonderful together."

"Do you know Chopin's Waltz in D flat?" Mrs. Eisenberg asked Mrs. Patrick. "Yes," Mrs. Patrick answered. The two women sat down at the piano and began to play. Mrs. Eisenberg used only her right hand, and Mrs. Patrick used only her left hand. The music sounded good. The women discovered that they loved the same music. Together they began to play the music they loved. They were not sad anymore.

Mrs. Patrick said, "Sometimes God closes a door and then opens a window. I lost my music, but I found Ruth. Now I have my music again. I have my friend Ruth, too."

2. VOCABULARY

Which words have the same meaning as the words in the story? Circle the letter of the correct answer.

1. Mrs. Patrick had a *stroke*. She couldn't move or speak.
   a. a serious sickness
   b. an idea

2. She got better, but her right side was still *weak*. She couldn't play the piano anymore.
   a. cold
   b. not strong

3. Playing the piano was Mrs. Eisenberg's *hobby*.
   a. something she did for money
   b. something she did in her free time

4. Mrs. Patrick and Mrs. Eisenberg *give concerts*.
   a. play the piano, and people listen
   b. speak, and people take pictures

3. COMPREHENSION

FINDING INFORMATION

Read the questions. Find the answers in the story. Write the answers.

1. Do Mrs. Patrick and Mrs. Eisenberg play the piano or the violin?

   They play the piano.

2. Are they famous because they play well or because they play with only one hand?

   _____

3. Was Mrs. Patrick a piano teacher or a math teacher?

   _____

4. Was playing the piano Mrs. Eisenberg's job or hobby?

   _____

5. Did the women meet at a restaurant or at a senior citizens' center?

   _____

6. Do the women love the same music or the same books?

   _____

MAKING INFERENCES

Read the sentences below. Some of the sentences are true, and some of the sentences are false. If a sentence is true, circle T. If a sentence is false, circle F. Which sentence from the story helped you? Copy the sentence.

1. Mrs. Eisenberg and Mrs. Patrick never travel.

   T (F) *They give concerts in the United States and in Canada.*

2. Mrs. Patrick's children can play the piano.

   T   F   _____

3. Only young people have strokes.

   T   F   _____

4. Mrs. Patrick loves the music of Beethoven, but Mrs. Eisenberg doesn't.

   T   F   _____

REVIEWING THE STORY

Do you remember the story? Complete each sentence. Then read the story again. Were you right?

Ruth Eisenberg and Margaret Patrick _____play_____ the piano
                                              1
together. Mrs. Eisenberg plays with only her right _____ ,
                                                          2
and Mrs. Patrick plays with only her _____ hand.
                                            3

Both women _____ the piano. Mrs. Patrick was a
                   4
piano _____ , and playing the piano was Mrs. Eisenberg's
            5
_____ . Then both women had a _____ .
      6   7
They could not play the _____ anymore.
                               8

They met at a senior citizens' _____ . They discovered
                                        9
that they loved the same _____ and that they could
                                 10
play together. Now they _____ concerts in the United
                                11
States and in Canada. They are often _____ TV. They
                                             12
_____ famous.
      13

4. DISCUSSION

Think about these questions. Discuss your answers with your classmates.

1. Mrs. Eisenberg and Mrs. Patrick love classical music—the music of Chopin, Bach, and Beethoven. What kind of music do you like?
2. What kind of music is popular in your country? Do you hear American music in your country? Which American songs and singers are popular?
3. Choose a cassette of music from your country. Bring the cassette to class. Find a song with words. Play the song for the class. Ask classmates who don't speak your language, "What is this song about?" Your classmates will make guesses about the song.

5. WRITING

Write about Mrs. Eisenberg and Mrs. Patrick.

1. _They play the piano together._
2. _____
3. _____
4. _____

1. PRE-READING

Look at the pictures.

- What is the woman doing in the first picture?
- Why are the people watching her?
- What happened to the woman in the second picture?

The Bed

IS it difficult for you to get up in the morning? Do you sometimes oversleep? Are you often late for work or school? Yes? Then Hiroyuki Sugiyama of Japan has a special bed for you. Hiroyuki's bed will get you up in the morning! Here is how it works:

The bed is connected to an alarm clock. First, the alarm clock rings. You have a few minutes to wake up. Next, a tape recorder in the bed plays soft music or other pleasant sounds. The tape recorder in Hiroyuki's bed plays a recording of his girlfriend. She whispers in a sweet voice, "Wake up, darling, please." A few minutes later, a second recording plays. The second recording can be loud music or unpleasant sounds. Hiroyuki hears a recording of his boss. His boss shouts, "Wake up immediately, or you'll be late!"

If you don't get up after the second recording, you'll be sorry. A mechanical "foot" is in the bed. The mechanical foot kicks you in the head. Then the bed waits a few more minutes. What! You're still in bed! Slowly, the top of the bed rises higher and higher. The foot of the bed goes lower and lower. Finally, the bed is vertical. You slide off the bed and onto the floor. You are awake and out of bed.

The woman in the pictures is demonstrating Hiroyuki's bed. In the first picture, the bed is rising a little. The woman is still sleeping. In the second picture, the bed is almost vertical. The woman is not sleeping anymore.

Hiroyuki made his bed because he wanted to win a contest. He works for Honda Motor Company. Once every two years, Honda has a contest—the "All-Honda Idea Contest." It is for Honda's 200,000 employees. The employees think of new ideas. If their ideas win, the employees win prizes. In 1986 Hiroyuki Sugiyama won a prize for his bed.

Hiroyuki wanted to win a prize. He also wanted to solve a problem. "Getting up in the morning is difficult for me," Hiroyuki said. "Often I am almost late for work. Maybe this bed will solve my problem."

Hiroyuki's bed is not in stores. There is only one bed—the bed Hiroyuki made for the contest. Maybe someday a company will make Hiroyuki's bed and sell it in stores. Maybe people will buy millions of beds. Then Hiroyuki will be rich. If the bed makes Hiroyuki rich, it certainly will solve his problem. Hiroyuki will have a lot of money. He won't need to go to work, and he won't need to get up early!

2. VOCABULARY

Read the sentences. Guess the meaning of the words. Circle the letter of the right answer.

1. The tape recorder plays soft music or other *pleasant* sounds.

   a. nice

   b. fast

2. His girlfriend *whispers* in a sweet voice, "Wake up, darling, please."

   a. speaks very quietly

   b. speaks very loudly

3. The top of the bed rises higher and higher. The foot of the bed goes lower and lower. Finally, the bed is *vertical*.

   a. ————— b. |

4. The woman in the picture is *demonstrating* the bed.

   a. making

   b. showing

3. COMPREHENSION

FINDING INFORMATION

Read the questions. Find the answers in the story. Write the answers.

1. Did Hiroyuki make a special bed or a special chair?

   He made a special bed.

2. Is the bed for people who can't sleep or for people who oversleep?

   _____

3. Is the bed connected to an alarm clock or to a TV?

   _____

4. Does the bed have a telephone or a tape recorder?

   _____

5. Does Hiroyuki work for Honda Motor Company or for Ford Motor Company?

   _____

6. Did Hiroyuki make the bed because he wanted to win a contest or because he works in a bed factory?

   _____

UNDERSTANDING CAUSE AND EFFECT

Find the best way to complete each sentence. Write the letter of your answer on the line.

1. _____ Getting up in the morning is a problem for Hiroyuki, so

2. _____ Hiroyuki wanted to solve his problem, so

3. _____ The bed is vertical, so

4. _____ Hiroyuki won the contest, so

5. _____ The bed is not in stores, so

a. he won a prize.

b. the sleeper slides off the bed and onto the floor.

c. he is often almost late for work.

d. you can't buy it.

e. he made a special bed.

UNDERSTANDING PRONOUNS

Look at the pronouns. What do they mean? Draw a line to your answer and circle the word or words.

Hiroyuki Sugiyama of Japan made (a special bed.) *It* is for people who
oversleep. The bed has an alarm clock and a tape recorder. *It* also has a
mechanical foot. The foot kicks people in the head.

The woman in the picture is demonstrating the bed. In the first picture
she is sleeping. In the second picture *she* is not sleeping anymore.

Hiroyuki made the bed because *he* wanted to win a contest. *He* also
wanted to solve a problem. "Getting up in the morning is difficult for *me*,"
Hiroyuki said. "Maybe this bed will solve my problem."

4. DISCUSSION

Ask a classmate these questions.

1. Do you need Hiroyuki's bed? Is getting up in the morning easy or
   difficult for you?
2. When do you usually go to bed? When do you usually get up?
3. Is getting up in the morning difficult for anybody in your family? How
   do you get him or her out of bed?
4. Some people are "morning people." They like to go to bed early and
   get up early. Other people are "night people." They like to stay up late
   and get up late. Are you a "morning person" or a "night person"?
5. In some countries people sleep in the afternoon. Do people in your
   country sleep in the afternoon? Do you like to sleep in the afternoon?
6. Hiroyuki is often almost late for work. Are you often late, or are you
   always on time?

5. WRITING

Hiroyuki made a new bed. The bed was Hiroyuki's invention. Do you
have an idea for an invention? Draw a picture of your invention. Give it a
name. What does your invention do? Write about it.

Here is an example.

*If you put on these glasses,
you will know your partner's feelings.*

CAMAHTA CMИT

1985

5^к ПОЧТА СССР

1. PRE-READING

Look at the picture.

- What language is on the postage stamp?
- Whose picture is on the postage stamp?

Dear Mr. Androopov

SAMANTHA Smith, a little girl from Maine, was frightened. On TV she saw programs about nuclear bombs. In news magazines she saw pictures of U.S. and Soviet missiles. Samantha decided to write a letter to Yuri Andropov, the leader of the Soviet Union. She wrote:

Dear Mr. Andropov,

My name is Samantha Smith. I am ten years old. I am worried about nuclear war between Russia and the United States. How are you going to help so we don't have a war? Please tell me.

I have another question, but you don't have to answer it. Why do you want to conquer the world or at least our country? God wants us to live together in peace and not to fight.

Sincerely,
Samantha Smith

A few months later, Samantha received a letter from Mr. Andropov. The letter said: "The Soviet Union doesn't want war with the United States. We want peace and friendship. Please visit my country. I want you to learn about the Soviet Union and to meet Soviet children. Summer is the best time to visit."

Samantha and her parents went to the Soviet Union in July 1983. Soviet guides took them to important and beautiful places. Samantha learned to sing Russian songs and dance Russian dances. Sometimes she wore traditional Russian clothes.

People in both the Soviet Union and the United States watched Samantha on TV. Samantha won their hearts. She was friendly and cheerful, a beautiful child with a big smile. Everyone liked her.

At a children's camp in the Soviet Union, Samantha became friends with Natasha, a Soviet girl. Natasha and Samantha swam together and played the piano together. They talked about music and clothes. Sometimes they talked about peace. Natasha said she didn't hate America and didn't ever want war. "Natasha and I are friends," Samantha thought. "Why can't our countries be friends?" Later Samantha wrote a book about her trip. On the first page she wrote, "I dedicate this book to the children of the world. They know that peace is always possible."

Two years after her trip, Samantha Smith died in a plane crash. She was thirteen years old. People in both the United States and the Soviet Union were very sad.

The Soviet people didn't want to forget Samantha. They put her picture on a postage stamp. They named a mountain, a flower, and a ship "Samantha Smith." When a Soviet astronomer discovered a new planet, he named it "Samantha Smith." The astronomer said, "Samantha lived a short life. But she shone very brightly in it."

---

2. VOCABULARY

Read the sentences. Guess the meaning of the words. Circle the letter of the right answer.

1. Samantha saw TV programs about nuclear bombs. She was *frightened*.
   a. surprised
   b. afraid

2. Samantha wrote Mr. Andropov, "God doesn't want us to fight. Why do you want to *conquer* the world?"
   a. help with money
   b. take by force

3. Samantha was friendly and *cheerful*, a beautiful child with a big smile.
   a. sad
   b. happy

4. An *astronomer* discovered a new planet.
   a. a scientist who studies the sun, moon, and stars
   b. a scientist who studies rocks, dirt, and mountains

3. COMPREHENSION

FINDING INFORMATION

Read the questions. Find the answers in the story. Write the answers.

1. Did Samantha receive a package or a letter from Mr. Andropov?

    She received a letter from Mr. Andropov.

2. Who took Samantha to beautiful places—Mr. Andropov or Soviet guides?

    _____

3. Did Samantha wear modern Russian clothes or traditional Russian clothes?

    _____

4. Did Samantha and Natasha swim at a camp or at a school?

    _____

5. Did Samantha dedicate her book to children or to adults?

    _____

6. Did the astronomer discover a new moon or a new planet?

    _____

UNDERSTANDING REASONS

Find the best way to complete each sentence. Write the letter of your answer on the line.

1. _____ Samantha wrote Mr. Andropov

2. _____ Mr. Andropov wrote Samantha

3. _____ People in both the United States and the Soviet Union turned on their TVs

4. _____ Samantha went to a children's camp

5. _____ The Soviet people put Samantha's picture on a postage stamp

a. to remember her.

b. to watch Samantha.

c. to meet Soviet children.

d. to invite her to visit the Soviet Union.

e. to ask him some questions.

REVIEWING THE STORY

Do you remember the story? Complete each sentence. Then read the story again. Were you right?

Samantha Smith wrote a ___*letter*___ to Yuri Andropov.
1

She wrote, "I am worried _____ nuclear war between
2

Russia and the United _____ . How are you going
3

_____ help so we don't have a _____ ?"
4   5

Mr. Andropov invited Samantha and her parents to _____
6

his country. In July 1983 they went to the _____ Union.
7

Samantha became friends with Natasha, a Soviet _____
8

Samantha thought, "We are friends. Why can't our _____
9

be friends?"

Samantha wrote a _____ about her trip to the Soviet
10

Union. On the first page she wrote, "I dedicate this book to the

_____ of the world. They know that _____
11   12

is always possible."

4. DISCUSSION

Soviet guides took Samantha to important and beautiful places. Imagine that a classmate is going to visit your country. You will be your classmate's guide. You will take your classmate to important and beautiful places. Draw a map of your country. Put the places that you will visit on the map. Show the map to your classmate. Tell your classmate about each place on the map.

5. WRITING

A. Write a letter to the leader of a country. Tell the leader your opinions.

B. Samantha learned that American girls and Soviet girls are alike in many ways. In what ways are Americans and people from your country alike? In what ways are they different? Write your answers.

Americans and people from my country are alike. For example:

Americans and people from my country are different. For example:

_____

_____

_____

_____

1. PRE-READING

Look at the picture.

- Who are these people?
- Where are they?
- Why does the boy look unhappy?
- Why does the man look angry?

Parents at School

TOM, a 13-year-old boy, was a student at a junior high school in Ohio. He was not a good student. He did not behave well at school. He talked in class, and he was often late. His teachers told him, "Go to the principal's office."

John Lazares was the principal at Tom's school. Tom went to Mr. Lazares's office. First Mr. Lazares disciplined Tom. He told him, "You have to stay at school an extra hour tomorrow." Then Mr. Lazares tried to talk to Tom. Tom didn't pay much attention. "He'll be back in my office soon," Mr. Lazares thought. He told Tom, "If your teachers send you to my office again, I'm going to call your mother. I'm going to say, 'The teachers are having problems with your son. Please come to school. I want you to go to classes with him.' "

Suddenly Tom sat up in his chair. "Oh, no!" he said. "Don't do that! I don't want my mother at school! I'll be good. I promise."

Later, Mr. Lazares thought about Tom's words: "I don't want my mother at school." "Hmm," Mr. Lazares thought. "Maybe I have a new way to discipline students."

In the United States, principals and teachers discipline students in several ways. The teacher often writes or calls the student's parents. Sometimes students have to stay at school for an extra hour. If a student behaves very badly, the principal can suspend the student. The student cannot come to school for one, two, or three days. Mr. Lazares didn't like to suspend students. When he suspended some students, they were happy. "A three-day vacation!" they thought.

A few days later, another boy was in Mr. Lazares's office. The boy was not behaving well in class. Mr. Lazares telephoned the boy's parents. "If you come to school with your son, I won't suspend him," he said. The boy's father came to school and went with his son to every class. Other students stared at the boy and his father. The boy was embarrassed. After that, he behaved better. He didn't want his father to come to school again. Other students behaved better, too. They thought, "I don't want *my* parents to come to school!"

That year about 60 parents came to school with children who didn't behave well. The next year only a few parents had to come to school. The students were behaving better.

Principals at other schools heard about Mr. Lazares's new way to discipline students. Now principals all over the United States are trying Mr. Lazares's idea. They, too, think that students behave better when parents come to school.

2. VOCABULARY

Complete the sentences. Find the right words. Circle the letter of your answer.

1. Tom talked in class, and he was often late. He did not _____ at school.
   a. read
   b. behave
   c. write

2. The principal told Tom, "You have to stay at school an extra hour tomorrow." The principal _____ him.
   a. helped
   b. saw
   c. disciplined

3. Students who behave very badly cannot come to school for one, two, or three days. The principal _____ them.
   a. visits
   b. suspends
   c. telephones

4. Other students stared at the boy and his father. The boy was _____ .
   a. frightened
   b. cheerful
   c. embarrassed

3. COMPREHENSION

UNDERSTANDING THE MAIN IDEA

Circle the letter of the best answer.

1. Another good title for this story is
   a. "The Boy Who Didn't Behave."
   b. "A New Way to Discipline Students."
   c. "Junior High Schools in the United States."
2. Students at Mr. Lazares's junior high school are behaving better because
   a. they are afraid of the teachers.
   b. Mr. Lazares suspends students who don't behave.
   c. they don't want their parents at school.

UNDERSTANDING CAUSE AND EFFECT

Find the best way to complete each sentence. Write the letter of your answer on the line.

1. _____ Tom didn't behave well at school, so

2. _____ Tom didn't want his mother at school, so

3. _____ Some students want a three-day vacation, so

4. _____ Other students stared at the boy and his father, so

5. _____ The other students didn't want their parents to come to school, so

a. he said, "I'll be good, I promise."

b. the boy was embarrassed.

c. his teachers sent him to the principal's office.

d. they behaved better.

e. they are happy when the principal suspends them.

UNDERSTANDING PRONOUNS

Look at the pronouns. What do they mean? Draw a line to your answer and circle the word or words.

(Tom) didn't behave at school, so his teachers sent *him* to the principal's
₁
office. Mr. Lazares told *him*, "*I*'m going to call your mother. *I*'m going to say,
₂ ₃ ₄
'The teachers are having problems with your son. *I* want *you* to go to classes
₅ ₆
with *him*.' "
₇

"Oh, no!" Tom said. "*I* don't want my mother at school! *I*'ll be good!"
            8   9

Mr. Lazares thought about Tom's words: "*I* don't want my mother at
                                        10

school!" "Hmm," Mr. Lazares thought. "Maybe *I* have a new way to discipline
                                              11

students."

Now when students at Mr. Lazares's school don't behave well, Mr. Lazares

doesn't suspend *them*. *They* have to bring their parents to school. Principals
                 12   13

at other schools are trying Mr. Lazares's idea. *They*, too, think that students
                                                 14

behave better when parents come to school.

4. DISCUSSION

Think about these questions. Discuss your answers with your classmates.

1. When students at Mr. Lazares's school don't behave well, their parents
   have to come to school. Is that a good idea or a bad idea?
2. What do students do when they don't behave well? (Do they make
   paper airplanes in class, for example?) Tell the class about a student at
   your school who didn't behave well. What did the student do?
3. Sometimes students cheat. For example, they look at another student's
   paper and copy the answers. Did students cheat at your school? How
   did they do it?

5. WRITING

Ask a classmate these questions about his/her elementary school.

1. How many children were in a class at your school?
2. Was the teacher strict or not strict?
3. How did the teacher discipline students who didn't behave well?
4. Did you behave well in school?

   You can write a paragraph from your classmate's answers.
   Here is an example.

   When Pedro went to school, there were about 50 children in the class. The teacher was very strict. When the students didn't behave, they had to stand in a corner of the classroom. Sometimes the teacher hit the students' hands with a ruler. Pedro was afraid of the teacher, so he behaved very well.

Now write your paragraph.

1. PRE-READING

Look at the picture.

- Where is this?
- What are the people doing?

Finders Keepers?

MEL Kiser was driving along a busy highway in Columbus, Ohio. He saw an armored truck a few cars ahead of him. Suddenly, the back doors of the armored truck opened, and a blue plastic bag fell out of the truck. A car in front of Mr. Kiser hit the bag. The bag ripped, and money spilled out. Then another bag fell out of the truck, and another. Soon money was flying everywhere.

"What are those green papers on the highway?" drivers wondered. "Are they leaves?" Then drivers realized that the green papers were not leaves— they were money! Drivers slammed on their brakes and stopped right in the middle of the highway. People jumped out of their cars and began to pick up money.

Mr. Kiser also got out of his car. He grabbed a plastic bag of money, put the bag in his car, and drove away.

Later Mr. Kiser counted the money. He had $57,000. For the next two hours, Mr. Kiser thought about the money. He needed a new furnace for his house. He wanted to take a vacation in Florida. He dreamed about spending the money. Then he went to the police station and returned the $57,000.

Mr. Kiser returned $57,000, and other people returned money, too. But over one million dollars were still missing. The armored truck company offered a 10% reward. "If you return $1,000, for example, we will pay you $100," the company said. Mel Kiser had returned $57,000, so the company gave him a reward of $5,700. More people returned money and got rewards. But over half a million dollars were still missing.

Then the armored truck company got some help. A man telephoned and said, "I was driving along the highway when I saw a traffic jam ahead. I didn't want to be in the traffic jam, so I took the next exit and got off the highway. Then I saw the money. People were running everywhere. I had a camera in my car and I took some pictures. Would you like the pictures?"

"Yes!" answered the armored truck company. The company gave the pictures to the police. The police looked closely at the pictures. They looked at the cars, the license plates, and the people's faces. They tried to find the people who had taken the money, but they didn't have much luck.

One man who had taken some money telephoned a Columbus newspaper. The man did not give his name. "I took two bags of money," he said. "I'm going to take the money and leave Columbus. I have enough money for the rest of my life."

2. VOCABULARY

Think about the story and answer the questions.

1. Bags of money fell from the *armored truck*. Do armored trucks carry things that are important or things that are not important?
2. After the bags *ripped*, were the bags closed or open?
3. After the money *spilled* out, was the money on the ground or in the bags?
4. Drivers *slammed* on their *brakes*. Did the drivers stop slowly or suddenly?
5. Mel Kiser *grabbed* a bag of money. Did he take the bag slowly and carefully, or did he take the bag quickly?
6. Do people use *furnaces* in hot weather or in cold weather?

3. COMPREHENSION

UNDERSTANDING DETAILS

Read the sentences. One word in each sentence is not correct. Find the word and cross it out. Write the correct word.

1. Mel Kiser was driving along a ~~quiet~~ *busy* highway in Columbus, Ohio.

2. He saw an armored bus a few cars ahead of him.

3. Suddenly the back doors of the armored truck closed.

4. A blue plastic cup fell out of the truck.

5. The bag ripped, and leaves spilled out.

6. Drivers wrote that the green papers were not leaves.

7. People jumped out of their houses and began to pick up money.

8. The armored truck company offered a 10% tax.

9. More people returned money, but over half a million pennies were still missing.

UNDERSTANDING TIME RELATIONSHIPS

Find the best way to complete each sentence. Write the letter of your answer on the line.

1. _____ When the back doors of the armored truck opened,

2. _____ When cars hit the plastic bags,

3. _____ When drivers realized that the green papers were money,

4. _____ When Mr. Kiser went to the police station,

5. _____ When the armored truck company offered a reward,

a. they slammed on their brakes.

b. the bags ripped.

c. blue plastic bags fell out of the truck.

d. more people returned money.

e. he returned $57,000.

MAKING INFERENCES

Read the sentences below. Some of the sentences are true, and some of the sentences are false. If a sentence is true, circle T. If a sentence is false, circle F. Which sentence from the story helped you? Copy the sentence.

1. There is not much traffic in Columbus, Ohio. T (F) *Mel Kiser was driving along a busy highway in Columbus, Ohio.*

2. When drivers saw the money, they did not drive very carefully. T F _____

3. The weather in Columbus, Ohio, is always hot. T F _____

4. Mel Kiser is an honest man. T F _____

4. DISCUSSION

Mel Kiser was honest. He returned the money. Are you always honest? Discuss these questions with a classmate.

1. What do you do when you buy something, and
   - the cashier gives you too much change?
   - the cashier says, "$10, please," but the price is really $11?
   - the cashier says, "$10, please," but the price is really $100?
2. What do you do when you find
   - a little money on the street?
   - a lot of money on the street?
   - a wallet with a name and address?
   - jewelry—a ring or a watch, for example?
3. Have you ever found money? How much did you find? Where did you find it? What did you do with it?

5. WRITING

Imagine that you lost something that is very important to you. Make a "LOST" sign. Describe what you lost. Write where you lost it. Offer a reward. Here is an example.

LOST
Gold Ring
Small woman's ring with 2 diamonds. Lost at the bus stop on 5th and Park Street. $50 reward for return. Please call 555-6554.

1. PRE-READING

Look at the picture.

- What does the man have on his face?

Good Bees and Bad Bees

THE killer bees are coming to the United States!

"Killer Bees" is not the name of a scary movie. Killer bees are real. They are bees that kill people and animals. And they really are coming to the United States.

The bees are coming from South America. They are slowly moving north and will arrive in the United States in the 1990s.

Killer bees are special bees. They are much more dangerous than regular honey bees because they sting more often than honey bees. And when killer bees sting, they often sting in groups. A group of killer bees sometimes surrounds a person, and then they all sting at the same time. The group can sting 400 or 500 times in one minute. Often the person dies. Killer bees have killed over 350 people in South America.

Killer bees, like honey bees, make honey. But they eat most of the honey themselves. They are not good for making honey because they are dangerous and difficult to control. To say it simply, honey bees are good bees, and killer bees are bad bees.

Scientists are working hard. They are looking for a way to stop the killer bees. It isn't easy because killer bees look like honey bees. Scientists don't want to kill honey bees by mistake.

In the picture, 100,000 bees are on the man's face. Are they killer bees, or are they honey bees? They are honey bees. They are not hurting the man; they are helping him. With the bees' help, the man won a contest.

The man, whose name is Max Beck, won a contest at a beekeepers' meeting. Every year beekeepers from all over the United States meet in New Jersey. At the meeting the beekeepers talk about bees, honey, and the killer bee problem. They also watch a contest. Some of the beekeepers attract bees to their bodies. The beekeeper who attracts the most bees wins the contest. In 1987 Max Beck won. He attracted 100,000 bees to his body.

Mr. Beck was not nervous with 100,000 bees on his body. Honey bees, like killer bees, sting. But they sting only when they are very frightened. Mr. Beck was careful not to frighten the bees. He moved very slowly and tried not to cough or sneeze. He said, "Not one bee stung me."

Beekeepers like Max Beck are worried about the killer bees. When killer bees come to an area, the honey bees in the area gradually change from honey bees to killer bees. Beekeepers can't use killer bees to make honey. They hope that scientists stop the killer bees soon. *Everybody* hopes that scientists stop the killer bees soon!

2. VOCABULARY

Think about the story and answer the questions.

1. Both killer bees and honey bees *sting*. When a bee stings, is it pleasant or painful?
2. Killer bees sometimes *surround* a person. Are the bees all around the person, or are they only behind the person?
3. To say it *simply*, honey bees are good bees, and killer bees are bad bees. When people say something simply, do they use words that are easy to understand or words that are difficult to understand?
4. Max Beck *attracted* 100,000 bees to his body. Did the bees fly to Max Beck, or did they fly away from Max Beck?
5. After Max Beck *won* the *contest*, was he happy or sad?
6. Max Beck tried not to *sneeze*. When people sneeze, do they cover their ears or their noses?

3. COMPREHENSION

UNDERSTANDING THE MAIN IDEA

Circle the letter of the best answer.

1. "Good Bees and Bad Bees" is about
   a. honey bees and killer bees.
   b. scientists who stop killer bees.
   c. a special contest.
2. Killer bees are bad bees because
   a. they look like honey bees.
   b. they don't help beekeepers win contests.
   c. they kill people and animals.

FINDING INFORMATION

Read the sentences below. If the sentence is true for killer bees, put a check (✓) under "killer bees." If the sentence is true for honey bees, put a check under "honey bees." If the sentence is true for both killer and honey bees, put a check under both "killer bees" and "honey bees."

	Killer Bees	Honey Bees
1. They sting.	✓	✓
2. They sting in groups.		
3. They have killed over 350 people in South America.		
4. They make honey.		
5. They eat most of their honey themselves.		
6. Scientists want to stop them.		
7. Beekeepers use them in a contest.		
8. Max Beck was careful not to frighten them.		

MAKING INFERENCES

Read the sentences below. Some of the sentences are true, and some of the sentences are false. If a sentence is true, circle T. If a sentence is false, circle F. Which sentence from the story helped you? Copy the sentence.

1. Killer bees are coming to Texas. (T) F *Killer bees are coming to the United States.*

2. Killer bees can kill a rabbit. T F _____

3. People in South America are probably afraid of killer bees. T F _____

4. Killer bees are orange and black, and honey bees are yellow and black. T F _____

5. Scientists who want to stop the killer bees work only three hours a day. T F _____

6. Max Beck is afraid of honey bees. T F _____

4. DISCUSSION

Think about these questions. Discuss your answers with your classmates.

1. Has a bee ever stung you? What happened? Do you have killer bees in your country?
2. Max Beck had 100,000 bees on his face. He won the contest. Would you put 100,000 bees on your face for $100? For $1,000? For $100,000?
3. The woman in the picture has a tarantula on her face. (Don't worry. The tarantula is dead.) Do you have tarantulas in your country? Do you have other big spiders? Are you afraid of spiders?
4. What kinds of big insects do you have in your country? Are these insects a problem sometimes?

5. WRITING

Write about killer bees.

1. *They kill people and animals.*
2. _____
3. _____

1. PRE-READING

Look at the picture.

■ How old are the children?
■ How did the boy hurt his forehead?

Children Who Don't Feel Pain

MR. and Mrs. Waters have two children. Their son, Paul, is two years old, and their daughter, Victoria, is six months old. Paul and Victoria are like most other children. But in one way they are very unusual. They almost never cry. They don't cry because they don't feel pain.

Paul Waters is like most two-year-olds. He runs and plays, and sometimes he gets hurt. But Paul doesn't know that he is hurt because he doesn't feel pain. He falls in the park and hurts his knee, but he gets up and continues running. He picks up a knife in the kitchen and cuts his hand, but he doesn't stop playing with the knife. His parents have to watch him every minute. Often they have to tell him, "Paul, stop playing. You're hurt."

Mr. and Mrs. Waters learned that Paul didn't feel pain when he was six months old. He had stomach problems, so his mother took him to the doctor. The doctor was afraid to touch Paul's stomach. "If I touch the baby's stomach, it will really hurt him," the doctor said. "I don't think so," Mrs. Waters said. "Paul almost never cries. I think he doesn't feel pain." The doctor touched the baby's stomach. Paul's mother was right. The baby didn't cry. Later,

when Paul was well, doctors did several tests. In one test, they put 60 small needles in Paul's neck, but Paul didn't cry. He didn't feel any pain.

Two years later, Mrs. Waters had a baby girl. "Will this baby have the same problem?" Mrs. Waters asked the doctors. "No," the doctors answered. "Paul's problem is very, very rare. Only four or five people in the world don't feel pain. Your daughter will probably be fine."

The Waters named their daughter Victoria. Soon they suspected that Victoria, like Paul, didn't feel pain. She cried only when she was hungry. She never cried when she was hurt. Sometimes, for example, Paul hurt her. Paul was like many big brothers. He was jealous of his baby sister. Sometimes he hit the baby's arm or hit her in the stomach. The baby just looked at Paul and smiled. Mr. and Mrs. Waters were worried. They took Victoria to the hospital for tests. After the tests the doctors told them, "Victoria doesn't feel pain, either."

Sometimes people tell Mr. and Mrs. Waters, "Your children don't cry? That's unusual!" "Yes," Mr. and Mrs. Waters say. "We have *very* unusual children."

2. VOCABULARY

Which sentences have the same meaning as the sentences in the story? Circle the letter of the correct answer.

1. Mr. and Mrs. Waters *learned* that Paul didn't feel pain when he was six months old.

   a. When Paul was six months old, his parents discovered that he didn't feel pain.

   b. When Paul was six years old, his teachers taught him about pain at school.

2. Paul's problem is very, very *rare*.

   a. Many people have Paul's problem.

   b. Not many people have Paul's problem.

3. Victoria never cried when she was hurt. Mr. and Mrs. Waters *suspected* that Victoria, like Paul, didn't feel pain.

   a. Mr. and Mrs. Waters thought, "Probably Victoria doesn't feel pain, either."

   b. Mr. and Mrs. Waters thought, "We know that Victoria doesn't like Paul."

4. Paul was *jealous* of his baby sister.

   a. Paul thought, "Everyone is looking at Victoria. I want people to look at me, too."

   b. Paul thought, "I don't want a baby sister. I want a baby brother."

3. COMPREHENSION

UNDERSTANDING THE MAIN IDEA

Circle the letter of the best answer.

1. The Waters children are unusual because
   a. they never get hurt.
   b. their parents watch them every minute.
   c. they don't feel pain.

2. Mr. and Mrs. Waters suspected that their children didn't feel pain because
   a. a doctor told them.
   b. the children almost never cried.
   c. many people don't feel pain.

UNDERSTANDING CAUSE AND EFFECT

Find the best way to complete each sentence. Write the letter of your answer on the line.

1. _____ Paul doesn't feel pain, so

2. _____ Paul had stomach problems, so

3. _____ Doctors wanted to test Paul, so

4. _____ Victoria cried only when she was hungry, so

5. _____ Paul was jealous of his baby sister, so

a. he doesn't know that he is hurt.

b. sometimes he hit the baby's arm.

c. her parents suspected that she didn't feel pain.

d. they put 60 small needles in his neck.

e. his mother took him to the doctor.

UNDERSTANDING PRONOUNS

Look at the pronouns. What do they mean? Draw a line to your answer and circle the word or words.

(Paul and Victoria) are very unusual. *They* almost never cry because *they* don't feel pain.
1   2

Paul's mother learned that Paul didn't feel pain when *he* was six months old. Paul had stomach problems, so his mother took *him* to the doctor.
3   4

The doctor was afraid to touch Paul's stomach. "*You* can touch his
                                                    5
stomach," Mrs. Waters told the doctor. "*He* won't cry. *I* think that Paul
                                             6   7
doesn't feel pain." Later doctors tested Paul. *They* put 60 small needles in
                                                 8
his neck. *He* didn't cry.
           9

Paul's sister Victoria has the same problem. *It* is very rare. Only a few
                                               10
people in the world feel no pain.

4. DISCUSSION

Think about these questions. Discuss your answers with your classmates.

1. The Waters children don't feel pain. Why is that good? Why is that
   bad? Would you like a life without pain?
2. The Waters children are very unusual. Do you know an unusual
   person? Tell your classmates about the person.

5. WRITING

What is unusual about you? Write a sentence about yourself on a small
piece of paper. Write something that your classmates don't know. For
example:

- Sometimes I dream about something, and then it really happens.
- I have 12 brothers and sisters.
- My father has a pet tiger.
- People think I am 18 or 19 years old, but I am 27.

**Give your paper to the teacher. The teacher will read all the sentences to
the class. Try to guess who wrote them.**

1. PRE-READING

Look at the picture.

- Where is the man standing?
- What is he holding?

The Museum of Failures

THE man in the picture is Robert McMath. Behind Mr. McMath are products you find in a supermarket. But Mr. McMath is not in a supermarket. He is in a museum.

Mr. McMath is the director of the "Museum of Failures," a special museum in New York. The museum has about 75,000 products that failed. The products were in stores, but not many people bought them. The companies stopped making the products, and they are not in stores anymore. Now they are in Mr. McMath's museum.

Mr. McMath is holding a can of "Silly String"— one product that failed. "Silly String" is a toy. Children push a button on top of the can, and a string of pink plastic comes out. The toy was popular for a short time. Children liked to play with the pink plastic string. They also liked to eat it! That was a problem. Parents stopped buying "Silly String," and the product failed.

Mr. McMath collects products like "Silly String" because his business is marketing. Mr. McMath knows a lot about selling products and advertising. He gives his clients advice about new products. Sometimes Mr. McMath shows clients around his museum. His clients can learn from the products that failed.

Products fail for many different reasons. Some fail because their names are not good. A few years ago a company made a new shampoo. The shampoo had yogurt in it, so the company named it "Yogurt Shampoo." The shampoo was not popular. Perhaps people thought, "Yogurt Shampoo? Is it something for my hair, or is it something to eat?" "Yogurt Shampoo" is now on a shelf in Mr. McMath's museum.

Another product in Mr. McMath's museum is mayonnaise in a tube. Americans didn't buy it. They thought, "Toothpaste comes from a tube. Mayonnaise comes from a glass jar." They didn't buy the mayonnaise because they didn't like the packaging.

Other products fail because the product itself is not very good. A few years ago, a company made a spray paint for bald men. The paint came in brown, black, and other colors. Men sprayed the paint on their heads. Of course, the paint didn't look like hair, and men stopped buying the paint. It is now in the "Museum of Failures."

Mr. McMath says that stores have more than 100 new products every week. About 20 percent of the new products are successful; the others fail.

A company in Britain is making an interesting new product. It is a pasta for children. Each piece of pasta is in the shape of a rat. Will "rat pasta" be successful? Or will it be one of the failures in Mr. McMath's museum?

2. VOCABULARY

Complete the sentences. Find the right words. Circle the letter of your answer.

1. The companies stopped making the products because not many people bought them. The products _____.
   a. grew
   b. failed
   c. fell

2. Mr. McMath knows a lot about selling products and advertising. His business is _____.
   a. marketing
   b. teaching
   c. cooking

3. Mr. McMath's clients ask him questions about marketing. He answers their questions and helps them. He gives his clients _____.
   a. advice
   b. money
   c. presents

4. About 80 percent of all new products fail; only 20 percent are _____.
   a. cheap
   b. successful
   c. interesting

3. COMPREHENSION

UNDERSTANDING THE MAIN IDEA

Circle the letter of the best answer.

1. "The Museum of Failures" is about
    a. popular toys for children.
    b. unusual names for new products.
    c. a museum for products that were not successful.
2. New products fail because
    a. they are often made of pink plastic.
    b. the name, the packaging, or the product is not good.
    c. they are too expensive for most people.

FINDING INFORMATION

Read the questions. Find the answers in the story. Write the answers.

1. Is Mr. McMath the director of a museum or a supermarket?

   He is the director of a museum.

2. Does the museum have 75 products that failed or 75,000 products that failed?

   _____

3. Did many people buy the products, or did few people buy the products?

   _____

4. Was "Silly String" popular for a short time or for a long time?

   _____

5. Did "Yogurt Shampoo" fail because the name was not good or because the packaging was not good?

   _____

6. Did mayonnaise in a tube fail because people didn't like the mayonnaise or because people didn't like the packaging?

   _____

7. Was the spray paint for bald men or for sick men?

   _____

8. Is "rat pasta" for rats or for children?

   _____

UNDERSTANDING PRONOUNS

Look at the pronouns. What do they mean? Write the letter of your answer on the line.

1. _____ *It* is in New York.

2. _____ *It* is Mr. McMath's business.

3. _____ *They* can learn from the products that failed.

4. _____ About 80 percent of *them* fail.

a. marketing

b. new products

c. Mr. McMath's clients

d. the "Museum of Failures"

4. DISCUSSION

Think about these questions. Discuss your answers with your classmates.

Do any American products seem very strange to you? Which American products do you like very much? Are there some products that you use in your country but cannot find in the United States?

5. WRITING

What do you like to do in your free time? Ask a classmate the questions below. Your classmate will answer "yes" or "no." Put a check (✔) under the answers.

	Yes	No
1. Do you like to go to museums?	___	___
2. Do you like to watch TV?	___	___
3. Do you like to eat at restaurants?	___	___
4. Do you like to play cards?	___	___
5. Do you like to shop for clothes?	___	___
6. Do you like to play soccer?	___	___
7. Do you like to read?	___	___
8. Do you like to listen to music?	___	___

Write your classmate's answers to the questions. For example:

1. Robert doesn't like to go to museums.
2. He likes to watch TV.

1. PRE-READING

Look at the picture.

- What is the woman doing with the money?
- Why is she doing that?

Money to Burn

LILLIAN Beard whistled and smiled while she worked. "Why are you so happy?" her co-workers asked her.

"Last week I got my income tax refund," Lillian answered. "This morning I went to the bank and cashed the check. I have $462 in my pocket. I'm thinking about the money. How will I spend it?"

After work, Lillian came home and decided to wash some clothes. She looked at the jeans she was wearing. They were dirty, so she put them in the washing machine, too. Ten minutes later she thought, "The money! It's still in the pocket of my jeans!" Lillian ran to the washing machine and took out the jeans. The money was still in the pocket, but it was wet. Lillian put the money on the kitchen table.

A few hours later the money was still wet. "Hmmm," Lillian thought. "How can I dry this money?" Then Lillian had an idea. She could dry the money in her microwave oven! Lillian put the money in the microwave, set the timer for five minutes, and left the kitchen.

When Lillian came back a few minutes later, she saw a fire in the microwave. She opened the oven door, blew out the fire, and looked at her money. The money was burned.

The next day Lillian took the burned money to the bank. A teller at the bank told her, "If I can see the numbers on the burned bills, I can give you new money." Unfortunately, the teller found numbers on only a few bills. The teller took those bills and gave Lillian $17.

A newspaper reporter heard about the burned money. He wrote a story about Lillian for the newspaper. Several people read the story and called the newspaper. "Tell Ms. Beard to send the burned money to the U.S. Department of Treasury," the people said. "Maybe she can get her money back."

Every year about 30,000 people send damaged money to the Treasury Department. Experts there look carefully at the damaged money. Sometimes they can give people new money for the damaged money. Once a farmer's cow ate his money—thousands of dollars. The farmer killed the cow and sent the cow's stomach, with the money inside, to the Treasury Department. The experts gave the farmer new money.

Lillian sent her money to the Treasury Department. The experts looked at Lillian's burned money and sent her a check for $231. What did Lillian buy with the money? She didn't buy anything. She gave the $231 to friends who needed money. Lillian said, "When I burned the $462, I thought, 'Well, my money is gone.' The check for $231 was a big surprise. I decided to give the money to my friends. Money is important, but people are more important to me."

---

2. VOCABULARY

Think about the story and answer the questions.

1. Do people *whistle* when they are happy or sad?
2. Do people pay *income tax* to the government or to the bank?
3. When people get a *refund*, do they receive presents or money?
4. Does a *microwave oven* cook food slowly or quickly?
5. Does a *timer* count minutes and seconds or dollars and cents?
6. Does a *teller* work at a supermarket or at a bank?
7. Does an *expert* know a little about something or a lot about something?

3. COMPREHENSION

FINDING INFORMATION

Read the questions. Find the answers in the story. Write the answers.

1. Did Lillian wash her jeans or her socks?

   She washed her jeans.

2. Was money in the pocket, or was candy in the pocket?

   _____

3. Did the money get old or wet?

   _____

4. Did Lillian put the money in her microwave oven or in her toaster?

   _____

5. Was the money delicious or was the money burned?

   _____

6. Did Lillian send her money to the Department of Treasury or to the Department of Education?

   _____

7. Did experts spend the money or look at the money?

   _____

8. Did Lillian get a check for $2,311 or for $231?

   _____

UNDERSTANDING PRONOUNS

Look at the pronouns. What do they mean? Write the letter of your answer on the line.

1. _____ Lillian cashed *it*.

2. _____ Lillian decided to wash *them*.

3. _____ Lillian set *it* for five minutes.

4. _____ *It* ate a farmer's money.

5. _____ *They* looked carefully at Lillian's burned money.

6. _____ Lillian gave *them* money.

a. experts at the Treasury Department

b. her income tax refund check

c. her jeans

d. the timer

e. a cow

f. friends

MAKING INFERENCES

Read the sentences below. Some of the sentences are true, and some of the sentences are false. If a sentence is true, circle T. If a sentence is false, circle F. Which sentence from the story helped you? Copy the sentence.

1. Lillian Beard works alone in an office.   T (F) *...her co-workers asked her.*

2. When people pay too much income tax, the U.S. government gives them money back.   T F _____

3. The teller at the bank found numbers on some one-dollar bills.   T F _____

4. Lillian had damaged money; that is very unusual.   T F _____

4. DISCUSSION

Think about these questions. Discuss your answers with your classmates.

1. Have you ever put money in a washing machine? Have you ever lost money in an unusual way? Have you ever found money in an unusual place? Do you have an interesting story about money?
2. Show the class some money from your country. U.S. bills are "dollars." What is the name of your country's money? What is the value of your country's money in dollars? Are pictures of people on the money? Who are the people?

5. WRITING

Look at a U.S. bill or coin. Whose picture is on the money? Go to the library and look in a history book, dictionary, or encyclopedia for information about that person. Then write three sentences. For example:

- Franklin Delano Roosevelt is on U.S. dimes.
- People called Roosevelt "FDR."
- Roosevelt was president for 12 years, from 1933 to 1945.

Now write your sentences.

1. _____

2. _____

3. _____

UNIT 19

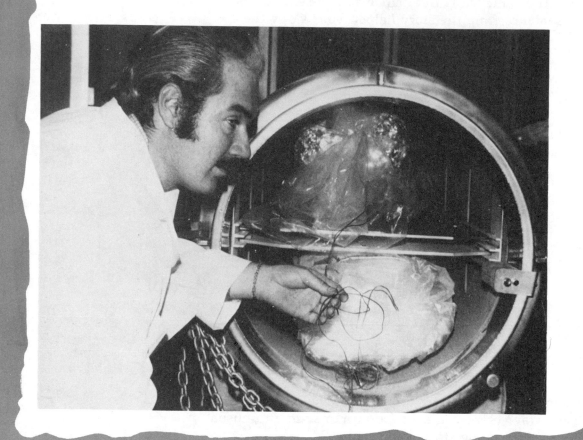

1. PRE-READING

Look at the picture.

- What is the man's job?
- What is he doing?
- What is inside the plastic bags?

A Chance to Live Again

THE man in the picture is Art Quaife. Art Quaife is a businessman. His business is freezing people. He works for a company in California called Trans Time. Trans Time freezes people after they die.

Why does Trans Time freeze people? Doctors today can cure many diseases, but they cannot cure all diseases. People still get sick and die. Maybe in the future doctors will have medicine for all diseases. Some people think so. They want Trans Time to freeze their bodies after they die. Maybe 100, or 200, or 300 years later, Trans Time doctors will bring the people back to life. The doctors will cure their diseases, and the people will be alive and healthy again.

Trans Time freezes people who die of disease. They also freeze people who die of old age. Maybe someday doctors will have medicine for old age. The Trans Time doctors will bring the old people back to life and give them medicine. The old people will be young again.

People often ask the scientists at Trans Time, "How will Trans Time bring dead people back to life?" The scientists answer, "We're not sure." In 1987 a Trans Time scientist froze a healthy dog. The dog's heart stopped beating; the dog was dead. Then, twenty minutes later, the scientist brought the dog back to life. Trans Time scientists say, "We can freeze a healthy animal and bring it back to life. We can't freeze dead people and bring them back to life. But we think that someday it will be possible." When the scientists say "someday," they mean years from now—maybe 100 or 200 years. How can Trans Time keep people frozen for 200 years?

After a person dies, workers at Trans Time cool the body with ice and chemicals. When the body is very cold, workers put the body into a capsule. They fill the capsule with liquid nitrogen. The temperature in the capsule is −196 degrees centigrade. Every two weeks workers add more liquid nitrogen. The liquid nitrogen keeps the bodies frozen. In the picture you can see two bodies in a capsule. Art Quaife is checking the temperature of the bodies.

Trans Time charges $21,000 to freeze a body and $59,000 to keep a body frozen. That's $80,000 all together. It's a lot of money. But some people think that $80,000 is a fair price. It's a fair price for a chance to live again.

2. VOCABULARY

Which sentences have the same meaning as the sentences in the story? Circle the letter of the correct answer.

1. Doctors today can *cure* many *diseases.*
   a. Today doctors give sick people medicine and send them to special hospitals.
   b. Today doctors give sick people medicine, and many of the sick people get well.

2. Every two weeks workers *add* more liquid nitrogen.
   a. Every two weeks workers put more liquid nitrogen into the capsule.
   b. Every two weeks workers count the capsules.

3. The liquid nitrogen *keeps* the bodies frozen.
   a. Trans Time does not give the bodies to other companies.
   b. With the liquid nitrogen, the bodies stay frozen.

4. Trans Time *charges* $21,000 to freeze a body.
   a. The cost of freezing a body at Trans Time is $21,000.
   b. People use credit cards when they pay Trans Time $21,000.

3. COMPREHENSION

UNDERSTANDING THE MAIN IDEA

Circle the letter of the best answer.

1. People want Trans Time to freeze their bodies because
   a. Trans Time's price is very low.
   b. they want to live again in 100, 200, or 300 years.
   c. freezing is good for their bodies.

2. After Trans Time brings people back to life, the people will be healthy because
   a. doctors will cure their diseases.
   b. they rested a long time.
   c. freezing cures diseases.

UNDERSTANDING DETAILS

Read the sentences. One word in each sentence is not correct. Find the word and cross it out. Write the correct word.

1. Art Quaife's business is ~~making~~ *freezing* people.
2. He works for a company in Illinois called Trans Time.
3. Trans Time freezes people before they die.
4. Teachers can cure many diseases, but they cannot cure all diseases.
5. Maybe in the past doctors will have medicine for all diseases.
6. They will have medicine for young age, too.
7. Trans Time doctors will bring people back to life and give them coffee.
8. The people will be alive and sick again.
9. Trans Time charges $21,000 to freeze a body and $59 to keep a body frozen.

UNDERSTANDING PRONOUNS

Look at the pronouns. What do they mean? Draw a line to your answer and circle the word or words.

People often ask (the scientists at Trans Time,) "How will *you* bring dead
1
people back to life?" The scientists answer, "*We*'re not sure." In 1987 a
2

Trans Time scientist froze a dog and brought *it* back to life. Trans Time
                                             3
scientists say, "*We* can freeze a healthy animal and bring *it* back to life.
              4   5
We can't freeze dead people and bring *them* back to life. But *we* think that
6   7   8
someday it will be possible."

---

4. DISCUSSION

Do you want Trans Time to freeze your body after you die? Why or why
not?

---

5. WRITING

Imagine that Trans Time freezes you and brings you back to life in 300
years. Write three sentences about the world you will see. For example:

- I will see people from other planets. People from earth will marry
  these people.
- Computers will do all our work.
- The earth will be one big country; there will be no borders.

Now write your sentences.

1. _____

2. _____

3. _____

1. PRE-READING

Look at the picture.

- Who are these men?
- What kind of work do they do?
- Why are they smiling?
- Where is Costa Rica on the map?

A Long Fishing Trip

ON January 24, 1988, Joel Gonzalez kissed his wife goodbye. Joel is a fisherman, and he was going on a short fishing trip. "I'll see you in a week," he said. But Joel did not see his wife in a week. He did not see his wife again for a long, long time.

Joel left his house and went to the harbor in Puntarenas, Costa Rica. He got on a fishing boat. Four other fishermen were on the boat, too. The boat left the harbor, and the men began to fish.

The first few hours on the ocean were not unusual. Then there was a terrible storm. The storm continued for 22 days. When the storm finally stopped, the men checked their boat. Their fishing nets were gone. The engine and the radio didn't work. There was no food, and there was no fresh water.

Without their nets, the men couldn't fish. But they could reach out of the boat and catch big turtles. The men didn't want to eat raw turtle meat, so they needed a fire for cooking. They tore down the boat's wood cabin and made a fire with pieces of the cabin.

They needed protection from the sun and rain, so they built a simple roof. The roof held rainwater, too. The men could drink rainwater from the roof.

For the next five months the men ate turtles—when they caught them. They drank rainwater—when it rained. Often there was no food and no water, and the men were hungry and thirsty. Sometimes they thought, "We are going to die soon."

Joel wrote a letter to his wife. "My dear Edith," Joel wrote. "If I die, I hope someone will send you this letter. Then you will know how I died. I had the best in life—a great woman and beautiful children. I love you, Edith. I love you."

In June it didn't rain for a long time, and the men ran out of water. They were thin and weak, and they thought, "We are going to die now." They put on their best clothes, lay down, and closed their eyes. After a while it began to rain. The men stood up and licked the water from the roof. Then all five men began to cry.

Ten days later, on June 15, a Japanese fishing boat found the men. They were 4,000 miles[1] from Costa Rica.

Nobody sent Joel's letter to his wife. He showed it to his wife himself. Joel will always keep the letter. The letter, he says, helps him remember. "On the ocean I realized that I love my wife and children very, very much. My family is everything to me. I don't want to forget that."

[1]6,437 kilometers

2. VOCABULARY

Think about the story and answer the questions.

1. Is a *harbor* for boats or for cars?
2. Do fishermen catch fish with *nets* or with *bags*?
3. Are *turtles* plants or animals?
4. Is *raw* meat cooked or uncooked?
5. The men tore down the boat's *cabin*. Which boat has a cabin—the boat in picture a. or the boat in picture b.?

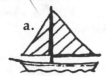
a.

b.

6. It didn't rain for a long time, and the men *ran out of* water. Did they have a lot of water or did they have no water?

3. COMPREHENSION

UNDERSTANDING REASONS

Find the best way to complete each sentence. Write the letter of your answer on the line.

1. _b_ The men left Puntarenas

2. _d_ The men reached out of their boat

3. _e_ Then the men tore down the boat's cabin

4. _c_ Joel wrote his wife a letter

5. _a_ Joel will keep his letter

a. to help him remember that his family is everything to him.

b. to fish in the ocean.

c. to tell her how he died.

d. to catch turtles.

e. to make a fire with the wood.

UNDERSTANDING PRONOUNS

Look at the pronouns. What do they mean? Draw a line to your answer and circle the word or words.

In January 1988 (five fishermen) went on a fishing trip. When *they* were 1 on the ocean there was a (storm). *It* lasted for 22 days. 2

After the storm the (men) checked their boat. First, *they* checked the 3 fishing (nets.) *They* were gone. Next *they* checked the (engine.) *It* didn't 4 5 6 work. Finally, *they* checked the (radio.) *It* didn't work either. 7 8

For the next five months the men ate turtles—when *they* caught *them*. 9 10 They drank (rainwater) when *they* had *it*. Often the (men) were hungry and 11 12 thirsty, and *they* thought, "*We* will die." 13 14

In June a (Japanese fishing boat) found the men. *They* were 4,000 miles 15 from Costa Rica.

MAKING INFERENCES

Read the sentences below. Some of the sentences are true, and some of the sentences are false. If a sentence is true, circle T. If a sentence is false, circle F. Which sentence from the story helped you? Copy the sentence.

1. Joel Gonzalez is single.   T (F)   *Joel Gonzalez kissed his wife goodbye.*

2. Joel Gonzalez wears a business suit to work.   T (F) _____

_____

3. Puntarenas is a city on the coast of Costa Rica.   (T) F _____

_____

4. Raw turtle meat is very delicious.   T (F) _____

_____

5. In January the sun is hot in Costa Rica.   (T) F _____

_____

4. DISCUSSION

Think about these questions. Discuss your answers with your classmates.

1. Joel Gonzalez is a fisherman. Do you fish sometimes? Do you catch big fish? Do you know any stories about fishermen or fishing?

2. Fishing can be dangerous work. Is your work dangerous? Is your work boring? What is the worst job you've ever had? What kind of work do you want to do?

5. WRITING

When Joel was far away from his wife, he wrote her a letter. Write a letter to a friend or relative who is far away. You can write about your English class, your family, your job, the weather, or your everyday life.

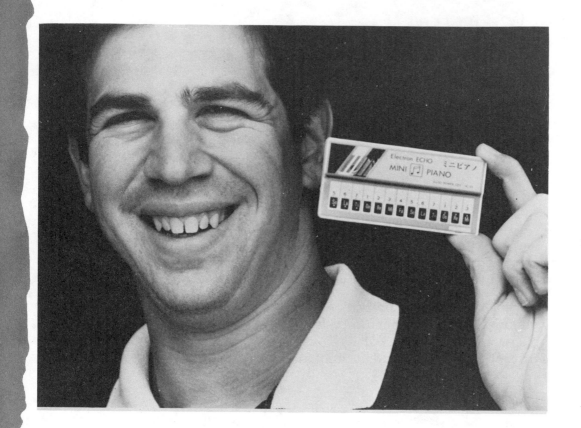

1. PRE-READING

Look at the picture.

- What is the man holding?
- Why is he smiling?

A Cheap Piano

ONE day Richard Brody got a letter from a company in New York. The company had good news for Mr. Brody. "Congratulations!" the letter said. "You are the winner of a mini electronic piano! Please send us $10 for shipping, and we will mail the piano to you."

A description of the piano was in the letter. Mr. Brody read the description very carefully and decided to mail the company $10 for the piano.

Two months later Mr. Brody received a box in the mail. It was his piano! He opened the box and found pieces of newspaper. He reached through the newspapers, . . . and reached . . . and reached. Finally, he felt something small and hard. He pulled out his piano. The piano was made of plastic and it was only five inches by two inches. It had 13 tiny buttons. When Mr. Brody pushed the buttons, the piano made a beeping sound. The piano costs $1.99 in most stores.

The company that sent Mr. Brody the piano was dishonest. Dishonest companies often do business by mail. They are very clever. They send letters and tell people that they have won something. They also trick people with their advertising.

One company sold "solar-powered clothes dryers" through the mail. The "clothes dryers" were cheap, so a lot of people ordered them. When the people received their "clothes dryers," they were disappointed and angry. The "solar-powered clothes dryer" was a string and a clothes pin.

Another company sold necklaces of "faux pearls." The necklaces were cheap, so a lot of people ordered them. Those people, too, were disappointed and angry when they received their necklaces. The "pearls" were made of white plastic. The people didn't know that in French *faux* means "not real." People ordered "faux pearls," and they got "faux pearls"—pearls that are not real.

Every year people in the U.S. send over 500 million dollars to dishonest companies. In the picture Richard Brody is laughing. He can laugh because he spent only $10 for his "mini electronic piano." Some people send much more than $10 to dishonest companies. Those people are not laughing.

The United States Postal Service tries to stop the dishonest companies who do business by mail. Three hundred employees at the Postal Service have only one job—stopping the dishonest companies.

The Postal Service employees give this advice: "If a company's prices are very, very low, watch out. Don't order a diamond for $5.99. And if you win a 'mini electronic piano,' don't send the company $10!"

2. VOCABULARY

Which words have the same meaning as the words in the story? Circle the letter of the correct answer.

1. Please send us $10 for *shipping*.
   a. sending the piano by mail
   b. putting the piano on a boat

2. Mr. Brody read the *description* very carefully.
   a. information that gives a picture with words
   b. business letter

3. The piano had 13 *tiny* buttons.
   a. round
   b. very small

4. One company sold "*solar*-powered clothes dryers."
   a. powered by gas
   b. powered by the sun

3. COMPREHENSION

UNDERSTANDING THE MAIN IDEA

Circle the letter of the best answer.

1. "A Cheap Piano" is about
   a. the U.S. Postal Service.
   b. pianos that cost $1.99 in stores.
   c. dishonest companies that do business by mail.
2. Dishonest companies
   a. make people happy.
   b. are not very clever.
   c. trick people with advertising.

UNDERSTANDING DETAILS

Read the sentences. One word in each sentence is not correct. Find the word and cross it out. Write the correct word.

1. Richard Brody paid $10 for a "mini electronic ~~guitar~~ *piano*."

2. The piano was made of wood, and it was only five inches by two inches.

3. The company that sent Mr. Brody the piano was honest.

4. Dishonest companies help people with their advertising.

5. The "solar-powered clothes dryers" were expensive, so a lot of people ordered them.

6. The "clothes dryer" was a machine and a clothes pin.

7. A lot of people ordered rings of "faux pearls."

8. The "pearls" were made of red plastic.

9. Every day people in the United States send over 500 million dollars to dishonest companies.

10. Postal Service employees give this advice: "If a company's prices are very, very high, watch out."

MAKING INFERENCES

Read the sentences below. Some of the sentences are true, and some of the sentences are false. If a sentence is true, circle T. If a sentence is false, circle F. Which sentence from the story helped you? Copy the sentence.

1. Mr. Brody paid too much
   for his piano. (T) F *The piano costs $1.99
   in most stores.*

2. The "solar-powered clothes T F _____
   dryers" cost $700. _____

3. The people who ordered T F _____
   "faux pearls" understood _____
   French very well.

4. Dishonest companies trick T F _____
   a lot of people. _____

5. A company is advertising T F _____
   air conditioners for $9.95. _____
   The company is probably
   dishonest.

4. DISCUSSION

Think about these questions. Discuss your answers with your classmates.

1. Has a dishonest company ever tricked you? What did you buy? What
   did you do?
2. Do people sometimes come to your house and try to sell you
   something? What do you say? Do people sometimes telephone you
   and try to sell you something? What do you say?

5. WRITING

**Read this story. It is in the present tense. Write the story again in the
past tense.**

Richard Brody gets a letter from a company in New York. The letter
says that Mr. Brody is the winner of a "mini electronic piano." Mr. Brody
has to send $10 if he wants the piano.

Mr. Brody reads the description of the piano very carefully. Then he
decides to send the company $10.

Two months later the piano arrives. Mr. Brody is disappointed. The
piano is made of plastic, and it is only five inches by two inches. It makes
a beeping sound. The piano is from a dishonest company.

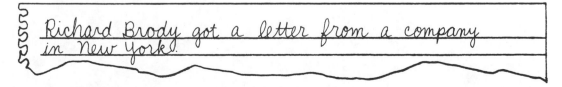

*Richard Brody got a letter from a company
in New York.*

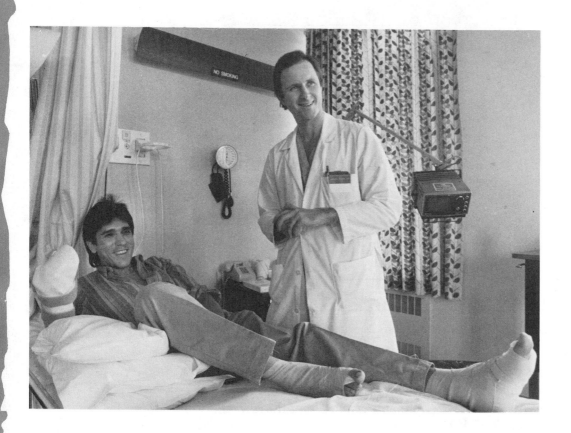

---

1. PRE-READING

Look at the picture.

- Where are the men?
- Who is the man in the white coat?
- Who is the man on the bed?
- What happened to the man?

A Surgeon Again

ON September 19, 1985, Dr. Francisco Bucio was getting dressed for work. His roommate, Angel Alcantara, was combing his hair. Both Francisco and Angel were doctors in Mexico City. They lived and worked together on the fourth floor of General Hospital. Suddenly the hospital began to shake. "Earthquake!" Francisco said. The hospital shook and shook. Then the hospital collapsed. Francisco and Angel fell four floors to the ground below. Three floors of the hospital fell on top of them. The doctors were trapped under a mountain of steel and concrete.

"Angel!" Francisco called to his friend. Angel moaned in pain. Then he was silent. Francisco knew that his friend was dead.

Francisco wanted to cry because Angel was dead. But he told himself, "Keep calm." Then he realized that his right hand was hurt. "Oh no, oh no," Francisco cried. "I can't lose my right hand. My right hand is my future."

For the next four days Francisco was trapped under the hospital. Every twelve hours Angel's watch beeped exactly at 7:30. "Angel's watch helped me," Francisco said. "I knew what day it was. But I wondered about my family. Were they safe? And I wondered about Mexico City."

On the third day Francisco became very thirsty. He dreamed of rivers with no water. He dreamed of ships on dry land.

Then, on the fourth day, rescue workers found Francisco. His right hand was trapped under concrete. The rescue workers wanted to cut off Francisco's hand. Francisco's brothers said, "No!"

When rescue workers carried Francisco out of the hospital, he still had his hand. But four fingers were badly crushed. Doctors had to cut off all four fingers on Francisco's right hand. Only his thumb remained. During the next months Francisco had five operations on his hand. His hand looked better, but it didn't work well. Francisco wanted to be a surgeon again. But he needed his right hand to operate on patients.

Then Francisco heard about a surgeon who was an expert in hand surgery. Six months after the earthquake the surgeon operated on Francisco. He cut off two of Francisco's toes and sewed the toes on Francisco's hand. The toes became new fingers for Francisco, and the new fingers worked well. Francisco could operate on patients. Dr. Francisco Bucio was a surgeon again.

"Now I know how patients feel," Dr. Bucio said. "I can sympathize and understand. I had six operations and so much pain, too much pain. Sometimes people joke. They say I'm the surgeon who operates with his feet. OK, my hand isn't beautiful, but I like it. It works."

2. VOCABULARY

Which sentence has the same meaning as the sentence in the story? Circle the letter of the correct answer.

1. The hospital *collapsed.*
   a. The hospital disappeared.
   b. The hospital fell down.

2. The doctors were *trapped* under a mountain of steel and concrete.
   a. A mountain of steel and concrete was on top of the doctors. They couldn't move.
   b. The doctors climbed a mountain of steel and concrete.

3. Angel *moaned* in pain.
   a. Angel made a sound because he was in pain.
   b. Angel closed his eyes because he was in pain.

4. "Now I know how patients feel," Dr. Bucio said. "I can *sympathize* and understand."
   a. "I understand patients' feelings and pain because I, too, had a lot of pain."
   b. "My patients are kind people, and I like them very much."

3. COMPREHENSION

UNDERSTANDING PRONOUNS

Look at the pronouns. What do they mean? Write the letter of your answer on the line.

1. _____ *He* was Dr. Bucio's roommate.

2. _____ *It* collapsed.

3. _____ *It* beeped every twelve hours.

4. _____ *They* were badly crushed.

5. _____ Dr. Bucio knows how *they* feel.

6. _____ *He* is the surgeon who operates with his feet.

a. his patients

b. the hospital

c. Angel's watch

d. Angel Alcantara

e. four of Francisco's fingers

f. Francisco Bucio

UNDERSTANDING TIME RELATIONSHIPS

Find the best way to complete each sentence. Write the letter of your answer on the line.

1. _____ When the hospital began to shake,

2. _____ When the hospital collapsed,

3. _____ When Angel's watch beeped,

4. _____ When Francisco slept,

5. _____ When the rescue workers wanted to cut off Francisco's hand,

a. Francisco said, "Earthquake!"

b. Francisco knew it was 7:30.

c. his brothers said, "No!"

d. he dreamed of rivers with no water.

e. Francisco and Angel fell four floors to the ground below.

MAKING INFERENCES

Read the sentences below. Some of the sentences are true, and some of the sentences are false. If a sentence is true, circle T. If a sentence is false, circle F. Which sentence from the story helped you? Copy the sentence.

1. General Hospital in Mexico   T (F) *Francisco and Angel*
   City is very small.   *fell four floors...*

2. When Francisco was   T   F   _____
   trapped under the hospital,   _____
   he had water with him.

3. During his four days under   T   F   _____
   the hospital, Francisco   _____
   slept sometimes.

4. Francisco Bucio is left-   T   F   _____
   handed.   _____

4. DISCUSSION

A. Think about these questions. Discuss your answers with your classmates.

Have you ever felt an earthquake? Where? When? What did you do?
Have you ever seen:

- a tornado?
- thick fog?
- a flood?
- hail?
- a snowstorm?
- a hurricane?

B. Francisco Bucio lives in Mexico. The weather in Mexico is warm and
dry. How is the weather in your country? Draw a map of your
country. Put your city on the map. Show the map to a classmate. Tell
your classmate about the weather in your city. Tell your classmate
about the weather in other parts of your country.

5. WRITING

Listen carefully when your classmate tells you about the weather in
his/her country. Then write a paragraph about the weather in your
classmate's country. Here is an example.

*Joko told me about the weather in Indonesia. It is always
warm in Indonesia. The equator goes through Indonesia.
North of the equator it is hotter than south of the equator.
It rains in Indonesia from October to March. The sun
shines from April to September.*

*Joko lives on the island of Java. He lives near the
beach, and the weather is always warm in his city.
It is cold here in Pennsylvania. I want to go to
Indonesia.*

Answer Key

UNIT 1

Vocabulary
1. c   2. a   3. c   4. c

Understanding the Main Idea
1. c   2. b

Understanding Cause and Effect
1. c   2. d   3. b   4. a   5. e

Reviewing the Story
1. disappeared   2. came   3. was   4. followed
5. swim   6. rested   7. island   8. girlfriend   9. about
10. distance   11. rough   12. famous   13. love

UNIT 2

Vocabulary
1. b   2. a   3. c   4. c

Understanding the Main Idea
1. c   2. b

Understanding Details
1. angry/afraid   2. money/help   3. party/wedding
4. boss/friend   5. angry/married   6. problem/trick
7. hospital/courthouse   8. telephoned/saw   9. Bob's/John's
10. boyfriend/husband

Understanding Cause and Effect
1. b   2. a   3. d   4. c

UNIT 3

Vocabulary
1. b   2. a   3. a   4. b

Understanding the Main Idea
1. b   2. c

Understanding Cause and Effect
1. b   2. d   3. c   4. a

Understanding Pronouns
1. d   2. a   3. b   4. e   5. c

UNIT 4

Vocabulary
1. He spoke loudly.   2. It makes a very loud sound.
3. She went with Rocco.   4. There were a lot of cars.

Understanding the Main Idea
1. b   2. b

Understanding Details
1. salesman/police officer   2. library/restaurant   3. woman/man
4. fixing/driving   5. hit/followed   6. 50/5
7. television/refrigerator   8. seat/door   9. light/heavy
10. mechanics/reporters

Understanding Reasons
1. d   2. a   3. c   4. e   5. b

UNIT 5

Vocabulary
1. a   2. a   3. b   4. b

Understanding the Main Idea
1. c   2. b

Understanding Details
1. China/Thailand   2. doctors/twins   3. laugh/stare
4. Australian/American   5. days/years   6. telephoned/met
7. unhappy/happy   8. can/can't

Understanding Reasons
1. d   2. c   3. a   4. b

UNIT 6

Vocabulary
1. a   2. b   3. a   4. a

Understanding the Main Idea
1. b   2. c

Finding Information
1. They live in Brazil.   2. She had a baby girl.   3. The baby got a number at the hospital.   4. They took their baby back to the hospital.   5. It is a city of seven million people.   6. The nurse gave Paulo the couple's address.   7. The hospital made a mistake.

Understanding Cause and Effect
1. e   2. c   3. d   4. a   5. b

UNIT 7

Vocabulary
1. c   2. a   3. b   4. a

Understanding the Main Idea
1. c   2. b

Understanding Time Relationships
1. a   2. c   3. b   4. d

Reviewing the Story
1. addicted   2. drug   3. smoking   4. gain   5. gum
6. little   7. chew   8. to   9. smoke   10. way

UNIT 8

Vocabulary
1. b   2. a   3. b   4. b

Understanding the Main Idea
1. b   2. c

Understanding Details
1. years/months   2. kitchen/yard   3. water/well
4. wrote/dialed   5. cover/hole   6. soft/solid   7. down/up
8. restaurant/hospital   9. old/young   10. rock/cover

Understanding Time Relationships
1. d   2. c   3. e   4. a   5. b

Writing
Jessica was playing at a day care center. Suddenly she fell into a well. She fell about 20 feet and couldn't get out of the well.

Men from the fire department came. They couldn't go down into the well because it was too narrow. The men decided to drill a hole next to the well.

For the next 58 hours, the men drilled the hole. Their job was very difficult because they were drilling through solid rock. Finally, they reached Jessica and brought her up from the well. Jessica's foot and forehead were badly injured, but she was alive. Everyone was very happy.

UNIT 9

Vocabulary
1. It has very small pieces of pearls.   2. They have eaten medicinal food for hundreds of years.   3. They use ginger often.
4. It helps the stomach.

Understanding the Main Idea
1. b   2. a

Understanding Details
1. furniture/food   2. backaches/headaches   3. beef/pearls
4. red/gray   5. delicious/medicinal   6. months/centuries
7. short/long   8. bakery/restaurant

Understanding Pronouns
1. d   2. a   3. b   4. c

UNIT 10

Vocabulary
1. a   2. b   3. b   4. a

Finding Information
1. They play the piano.   2. They are famous because they play with only one hand.   3. She was a piano teacher.   4. It was Mrs. Eisenberg's hobby.   5. They met at a senior citizens' center.
6. They love the same music.

Making Inferences
1. F   They give concerts in the United States and in Canada.
2. T   She taught her own children, too.   3. F   Then, when she was 69 years old, Mrs. Patrick had a stroke./Then, when she was 80 years old, she, too, had a stroke.   4. F   The women discovered that they loved the same music.

Reviewing the Story
1. play   2. hand   3. left   4. love   5. teacher
6. hobby   7. stroke   8. piano   9. center   10. music
11. give   12. on   13. are

UNIT 11

Vocabulary
1. a   2. a   3. b   4. b

Finding Information
1. He made a special bed.   2. It is for people who oversleep.
3. It is connected to an alarm clock.   4. It has a tape recorder.
5. He works for Honda Motor Company.   6. He made the bed because he wanted to win a contest.

Understanding Cause and Effect
1. c   2. e   3. b   4. a   5. d

Understanding Pronouns
1. a special bed   2. the bed   3. the woman (in the picture)
4. the woman (in the picture)   5. Hiroyuki   6. Hiroyuki
7. Hiroyuki

UNIT 12

Vocabulary
1. b   2. b   3. b   4. a

Finding Information
1. She received a letter from Mr. Andropov.   2. Soviet guides took her to beautiful places.   3. She wore traditional Russian clothes.   4. They swam at a camp.   5. She dedicated her book to children.   6. He discovered a new planet.

Understanding Reasons
1. e   2. d   3. b   4. c   5. a

Reviewing the Story
1. letter   2. about   3. States   4. to   5. war   6. visit
7. Soviet   8. girl   9. countries   10. book   11. children
12. peace

UNIT 13

Vocabulary
1. b   2. c   3. b   4. c

Understanding the Main Idea
1. b   2. c

Understanding Cause and Effect
1. c   2. a   3. e   4. b   5. d

Understanding Pronouns
1. Tom   2. Tom   3. Mr. Lazares   4. Mr. Lazares
5. Mr. Lazares   6. mother   7. your son   8. Tom
9. Tom   10. Tom   11. Mr. Lazares   12. students (at Mr. Lazares's school)   13. students (at Mr. Lazares's school)
14. principals at other schools

UNIT 14

Vocabulary
1. They carry things that are important.   2. They were open.
3. It was on the ground.   4. They stopped suddenly.   5. He
took the bag quickly.   6. They use furnaces in cold weather.

Understanding Details
1. quiet/busy   2. bus/truck   3. closed/opened   4. cup/bag
5. leaves/money   6. wrote/realized   7. houses/cars
8. tax/reward   9. pennies/dollars   10. pay/find

Understanding Time Relationships
1. c   2. b   3. a   4. e   5. d

Making Inferences
1. F   Mel Kiser was driving along a busy highway in Columbus,
Ohio.   2. T   Drivers slammed on their brakes and stopped
right in the middle of the highway.   3. F   He needed a new
furnace for his house.   4. T   Mr. Kiser returned $57,000.

UNIT 15

Vocabulary
1. It is painful.   2. They are all around the person.   3. They
use words that are easy to understand.   4. They flew to Max
Beck.   5. He was happy.   6. They cover their noses.

Understanding the Main Idea
1. a   2. c

Finding Information
1. killer bees and honey bees   2. killer bees   3. killer bees
4. killer bees and honey bees   5. killer bees   6. killer bees
7. honey bees   8. honey bees

Making Inferences
1. T   Killer bees are coming to the United States.   2. T   They
are bees that kill people and animals.   3. T   Killer bees have
killed over 350 people in South America.   4. F   Killer bees
look like honey bees.   5. F   Scientists are working hard.
6. F   Mr. Beck was not nervous with 100,000 bees on his body.

UNIT 16

Vocabulary
1. a   2. b   3. a   4. a

Understanding the Main Idea
1. c   2. b

Understanding Cause and Effect
1. a   2. e   3. d   4. c   5. b

Understanding Pronouns
1. Paul and Victoria   2. Paul and Victoria   3. Paul   4. Paul
5. the doctor   6. Paul   7. Mrs. Waters   8. doctors
9. Paul   10. problem

UNIT 17

Vocabulary
1. b   2. a   3. a   4. b

Understanding the Main Idea
1. c   2. b

Finding Information
1. He is the director of a museum.   2. It has 75,000 products
that failed.   3. Few people bought the products.   4. It was
popular for a short time.   5. It failed because the name was not
good.   6. It failed because people didn't like the packaging.
7. It was for bald men.   8. It is for children.

Understanding Pronouns
1. d   2. a   3. c   4. b

UNIT 18

Vocabulary
1. They whistle when they are happy.   2. They pay income tax
to the government.   3. They receive money.   4. It cooks food
quickly.   5. It counts minutes and seconds.   6. A teller works
at a bank.   7. An expert knows a lot about something.

Finding Information
1. She washed her jeans.   2. Money was in the pocket.
3. It got wet.   4. She put the money in her microwave oven.
5. It was burned.   6. She sent her money to the Treasury
Department.   7. They looked at the money.   8. She got a check
for $231.

Understanding Pronouns
1. b   2. c   3. d   4. e   5. a   6. f

Making Inferences
1. F   . . . her co-workers asked her.   2. T   "Last week I got
my income tax refund."   3. T   The teller gave Lillian $17.
4. F   Every year about 30,000 people send damaged money to
the Treasury Department.

UNIT 19

Vocabulary
1. b   2. a   3. b   4. a

Understanding the Main Idea
1. b   2. a

Understanding Details
1. making/freezing   2. Illinois/California   3. before/after
4. teachers/doctors   5. past/future   6. young/old
7. coffee/medicine   8. sick/healthy   9. $57/$59,000

Understanding Pronouns
1. the scientists at Trans Time   2. the scientists   3. dog
4. Trans Time scientists   5. a healthy animal   6. Trans Time
scientists   7. dead people   8. Trans Time scientists

UNIT 20

Vocabulary
1. It is for boats.   2. They catch fish with nets.   3. They are animals.   4. It is uncooked.   5. The boat in picture b has a cabin.   6. They had no water.

Understanding Reasons
1. b   2. d   3. e   4. c   5. a

Understanding Pronouns
1. five fishermen   2. storm   3. the men   4. the fishing nets   5. the men   6. the engine   7. the men   8. the radio   9. the men   10. turtles   11. the men   12. rainwater   13. the men   14. the men   15. the men

Making Inferences
1. F   Joel Gonzalez kissed his wife goodbye.   2. F   Joel is a fisherman.   3. T   Joel left his house and went to the harbor in Puntarenas, Costa Rica.   4. F   The men didn't want to eat raw turtle meat . . .   5. T   They needed protection from the sun . . .

UNIT 21

Vocabulary
1. a   2. a   3. b   4. b

Understanding the Main Idea
1. c   2. c

Understanding Details
1. guitar/piano   2. wood/plastic   3. honest/dishonest   4. help/trick   5. expensive/cheap   6. machine/string   7. rings/necklaces   8. red/white   9. day/year   10. high/low

Making Inferences
1. T   The piano costs $1.99 in most stores.   2. F   The "clothes dryers" were cheap.   3. F   The people didn't know that in French *faux* means "not real."   4. T   Every year people in the U.S. send over 500 million dollars to dishonest companies.   5. T   "If a company's prices are very, very low, watch out."

Writing
Richard Brody got a letter from a company in New York. The letter said that Mr. Brody was the winner of a "mini electronic piano." Mr. Brody had to send $10 if he wanted the piano.

Mr. Brody read the description of the piano very carefully. Then he decided to send the company $10.

Two months later the piano arrived. Mr. Brody was disappointed. The piano was made of plastic, and it was only five inches by two inches. It made a beeping sound. The piano was from a dishonest company.

UNIT 22

Vocabulary
1. b   2. a   3. a   4. a

Understanding Pronouns
1. d   2. b   3. c   4. e   5. a   6. f

Understanding Time Relationships
1. a   2. e   3. b   4. d   5. c

Making Inferences
1. F   Francisco and Angel fell four floors . . .   2. F   Francisco became very thirsty.   3. T   He dreamed of rivers with no water.   4. F   But he needed his right hand to operate on patients.

ACKNOWLEDGMENTS

I wish to thank:

- my husband, John, who introduced me to word processing and who managed to find every paragraph I lost;
- Sharron Bassano, who shared her wonderful collection of interactive activities;
- my editor, Penny Laporte, who, as a former ESL teacher, improved the stories and exercises so that they worked better in the classroom as well as on the printed page;
- Lori Coleman, Alice Muller, Cathy Diaz, and Nanda Wilson, who field-tested materials at the Santa Cruz, California, Adult School;
- my students at the American Language Institute at IUP, with whom I field-tested stories and exercises;
- Akiya Miyazato, editor-in-chief of *The Ryukyu Shimpo*, Arthur Porter, editor of the *Bridlington Free Press*, and the many newspaper librarians and reporters who provided clippings, photos, and leads;
- librarians Susan Karatjas and Rita Brode at the Indiana Free Library, who helped with research;
- the reference librarians at Stapleton Library, IUP, who provided many names and addresses;
- Ichiro Tabeshita, Yuko Yamagishi, Hiroko Mizumori, and Kaoru Nakahori, who translated materials for "Puppy Love";
- Zilda de Moura and Sharon Miranda, who translated materials for "The Baby Exchange";
- Hong Kun and Zhang Xiaolin, who offered their viewpoints on Chinese medicinal food;
- Margaret Patrick, who sent her collection of clippings;
- Bret Anderson and Hiroyuki Sugiyama of Honda Corporation, who provided information for "The Bed";
- John Lazares, who sent his videos and clippings about his "Parents at School" program;
- Norm Gary of the University of California at Davis, who provided up-to-date information on Africanized honey bees;
- Robert McMath, who sent his collection of clippings about the "Museum of Failures";
- Richard Brody, who good-naturedly agreed to share his experience with mail fraud;
- Cyrus Rowshan, who helped with the photography.